Goodbye Again

Goodbye Again

EXPERIENCES WITH DEPARTED LOVED ONES

By Edie Devers, Ph.D.

Andrews and McMeel
A Universal Press Syndicate Company
Kansas City

Goodbye Again: Experiences with Departed Loved Ones
copyright © 1997 by Edie Devers.
All rights reserved. Printed in the United States of America.
No part of this book may be used or reproduced in any manner
whatsoever without written permission except in the case of
reprints in the context of reviews. For information, write
Andrews and McMeel, a Universal Press Syndicate Company,
4520 Main Street, Kansas City, Missouri 64111.

Library of Congress Cataloging-in-Publication Data
Devers, Edie.
Goodbye again: experiences with departed loved ones / Edie
Devers.
p.   cm.
Includes bibliographical references.
ISBN 0-8362-2154-0
1. Spiritualism.   I. Title.
BF1261.2.D48   1997
133.9—dc21   96-37723
                                              CIP

This book is dedicated to my parents.

Contents

Contents

Acknowledgments

I am grateful to my family and friends for all the help and support they gave me in so many diverse ways.

I want to thank Sally Hutchinson, Ph.D., and the members of my research committee for their encouragement.

I want to acknowledge my literary agent, David Hendin, for asking me to turn my research into a book for the public.

Special thanks to the people at Andrews and McMeel, Jean Lowe and Rick Hill. I also want to warmly acknowledge Sandy Ghellis-Cole for her editorial assistance.

Last but not least, I want to thank all the people who participated in the research for giving so freely of their time and wisdom to help others understand this phenomenon.

Goodbye Again

Introduction

Two years after our mother died, my sister shared a most unusual story with me. A strange light had appeared to her, and in some inexplicable way it held within it the spirit of our deceased mother. It was not a ghost. She described it more as an embodiment of a positive thought form. From that day forward I witnessed a most remarkable change in my sister that made me believe the light had held powerful healing properties and a message filled with hope and love. What I did not know then, but I see clearly now, is that this light that had so miraculously transformed my sister's life would alter the course of mine as well.

Three years later while I was working on my master's degree in nursing, I happened on a newspaper article that described widows who saw and heard their deceased husbands. A shiver ran down my spine—the stories were so similar to my sister's. Clearly something of significance was at work here.

Since the experiences of the widows were described in the context of grief, I believed this phenomenon would be an acceptable topic for nursing research and despite the unusualness of my choice, I received a lot of support from my thesis committee. So in 1985 I began collecting data. I conducted a qualitative study that allowed me to look at the phenomenon from the research participant's perspective, and in a sense, enter his or her world. I answered the question: What is it like to experience the deceased?

During the next few years while maintaining a private psychotherapy practice and teaching nursing at a local university, I continued to read articles and to listen attentively to people who wanted to tell me about their experiences, and when appropriate, took field notes. When we discussed death-related topics in class or in the hospital setting, I would mention my research. It was not unusual for students or staff to reveal their own experiences. One student talked about how her twin brother, who had died in a boating accident, came to her a few nights after his death. She saw him sitting at the edge of her bed. He looked like a holographic image, but otherwise, just as she remembered him. He smiled and reassured her that she was on the right career path and told her he was there if she needed him.

Surprisingly, finding people who would share their experiences was much easier than I had anticipated. Students and patients willingly told their stories, as did others. Sometimes someone would spontaneously relate an encounter. While working on my thesis, I was at a copy service and the woman making copies of my interview questions paused and began reading the questions. She then smiled and told me of her experience with her father.

In 1989, when the time came to choose a dissertation topic for my Ph.D. in nursing, I chose the same topic but used a different qualitative research method to examine another aspect of this phenomenon. I wanted to understand the process that survivors went through during and after this remarkable experience. I now included in my evolving definition of after death experience dreams and sensing a presence, as well as awareness through one or more of the five senses.

In my private therapy practice, I continued to find opportunities to use and explore my growing knowledge about after-death communications (ADC), a term coined by Bill Guggenheim and Judy Guggenheim. Most of my patients have problems with depression or anxiety, and quite a number have grief-related problems. A few come to therapy specifically to deal with grief. Through my research I have come to recognize a significant correspondence between depression and anxiety and problems related to processing grief. And since I have seen a high frequency of ADCs, I regularly inquire whether or not a patient's current state of mind may be related to any "unusual" experience. This dialogue leads inevitably to the question: Have you had contact with the deceased or had any other unusual experiences that you want to discuss? We can then talk about the experience itself and any unresolved issues the survivor has with the person who has died.

MIRANDA

In therapy, Miranda was relieved to be able to talk about her experiences with her deceased mother. The first time she saw her mother Miranda was at home reading. It had been a long day at work, and Miranda had come in after dark. She was tired, so she stretched out on the sofa to read a magazine. She said that she noticed a certain stillness in the house. Then she looked up and saw her mother standing in the doorway between the living room and the kitchen. Her mother looked almost transparent, but Miranda could see faint color in her dress and hair. "She did not say anything. She just looked at me. She used to look at me like that whenever she was proud of something I'd done. She had this little half smile. We looked at each other for a minute or so and then she faded out. I felt close to her and peaceful while it was going on. Even though it sounds weird, it seemed perfectly normal." Miranda saw her mother on two more occasions. Each time was similar.

In therapy, we examined the meaning of the experiences and how they related to her grief and to her relationship to her mother, who had been a warm and nurturing woman. Miranda felt angry to be left without her, and we talked about what she could communicate to her mother spiritually to help deal with her anger over her mother's death. In time Miranda was able to tell her mother that she was angry but that she understood that her mother was ready to die. Miranda also promised to take better care of herself now and assured her mother that she would be all right.

Through my research and my work as a nurse/psychotherapist, I became aware of how important it is for bereaved people to be able to share all their thoughts, feelings, and experiences, no matter how unusual they may seem. Establishing a connection to others during grief is essential. It is far too easy for bereaved people to feel alone in the depths of grief. And if they believe others will not be understanding, they can feel further alienated. I have wanted my patients to feel free to discuss all their concerns without the fear of judgment.

I was also becoming more aware of how common ADC is. Though most accept their experiencing of ADC as normal, they think that other people will not understand, so they selectively disclose their experiences. I was saddened to see people treating this extraordinary and significant event in their grief work as if it were stigmatizing.

ADC is far from stigmatizing because it has both psychological and spiritual significance. It is psychologically significant because it helps to heal grief and provides a vehicle for resolving relationships with the deceased.

ADC has spiritual significance because it affirms that the physical and spiritual realms are not that separate. It makes people feel closer to those who have died and makes the spiritual world seem more accessible. ADC also confirms hope in life after death.

This book shares what I have learned from the data I have collected over the past ten years. I want to describe the depth and breadth of ADC but also communicate the meaning, power, and healing that such events can provide. I believe that this information is valuable to all who have contact with grieving individuals, whether families, friends, or professionals, as well as to those who are interested in this phenomenon. Though ADC can not be proven "real" through current quantitive means, it is a real phenomenon for those who have experienced ADC. As one participant in my research said, "I know what I saw was real, and it has changed my whole view of what death is all about."

I have changed the names of most of the people in this book. In some instances I have used composites in order to protect the privacy of the people who generously shared their experiences and to bring the events to life without compromising the integrity of my research.

Because the examples in this book describe the experiences between the living and the deceased, I will not repeat in each case that someone is the deceased; rather I will identify the deceased by the relationship he or she had with the living person. So, for instance, if a young woman describes seeing her brother standing at the foot of the bed, it should be assumed that her brother is the deceased.

One

Discovering After-Death Communication

Like my father, my sister was a hardened skeptic. If you couldn't prove something through quantitative science, it didn't exist. Years of undergraduate studies in behavioral psychology and a master's degree from Harvard University taught her to think like a detective. She ferreted out the "truth" with the tenacity of a pit bull. Mention a double-blind, placebo-controlled study and you had something to say, but slip in an assumption and you'd best prepare to defend yourself.

Then our mother died, and all that changed.

As my sister explains it, two years after our mother's death, she awoke abruptly to an inexplicable light. It shimmered and danced outside her window. At first, it reminded her of a strange fluorescent plankton she had once seen in the night waters off the coast of Florida. She couldn't identify what she was looking at until something even stranger happened.

Within this shimmering light pattern, my sister sensed a message, something she could only describe as a thought form. It said, "I'm doing fine. And so are you." It didn't need to say more. My sister knew in that instant it was our mother, and she had come to say goodbye again.

From that day forward, I witnessed a profound change in her. She was more at peace than I'd ever seen her before. Since that moment, a larger truth had been revealed to her, a truth that transcended her limited scientific way of knowing. Her worldview now embraced many possibilities that filled her with awe and wonder.

Years later my sibling still counts this extraordinary experience as a turning point in her life. She says, "After that, things just got easier. Life wasn't such a struggle. It's almost as if the chemical makeup of my brain changed."

Clearly, something mysterious had happened. My sister was not one to exaggerate. In fact, she had been the consummate skeptic. But suddenly she now entertained the thought of an unseen world and of contact with loved ones from that world. Yet she continued to be grounded in every other way.

What struck me most about my sister's experience was its power to instantly shift her worldview or paradigm. This sudden shift had a healing quality because it created a sense of awe, wonder, and hope. It also gave her a mental resiliency that had not previously existed. This resiliency brings to mind the comparison so often cited in Taoism of the mighty oak and the sapling. The sapling's ability to twist and turn in the wind gives it a strength the rigid oak has forgotten. In today's information age, mental flexibility is crucial. With new information challenging one's worldview almost daily, keeping an open mind facilitates mental health. In comparison, clinging rigidly to one worldview can threaten a person's very sense of self and mental balance. A personal paradigm shift facilitates open-mindedness because it dramatically illustrates the existence of multiple worldviews.

My sister rarely spoke of her extraordinary experience, but this experience set the stage for my doctoral research and my ten-year journey to discover more about this life-altering phenomenon. In the course of my research, I would learn a wealth of information about contact with the deceased and perhaps, most surprising of all, I would learn that this phenomenon is remarkably common. In this book I will share with you how ADC has impacted the lives of ordinary people and how one day it may impact your life, if it hasn't already.

Through in-depth interviews with survivors who have experienced deceased loved ones, I have been able to glimpse into people's private realities, which differ radically from their public personas. Just as my sister was reluctant to share her experience publicly, so too are most people. It is an understatement to say contact with the deceased carries a stigma. Not long ago, many spoke of such occurrences at the risk of excommunication, exile, or even punishment by death. People's reluctance to share this common experience is quite understandable.

While today societal punishment differs, it is still dramatic. The bereaved may be labeled insane and, in extreme cases, even medicated for psychosis. The bereaved may also be shunned socially and, at the very least, scoffed at in private. When I discovered through my literature reviews that a significant number of Americans experienced the deceased, I knew I must reveal this phenomenon for what it is. But what is it?

Some things I knew from my thesis. I knew ADC was normal, even healthy. But much remained elusive. The goal of my doctoral dissertation then became to systematically unravel this mystery, to uncover defining characteristics of this phenomenon, and to remove the stigma associated with it. As I spoke to the bereaved, fascinating patterns emerged that said a great deal about the resiliency of the human spirit and about our powerful, undying connection to loved ones. I also learned that behind the simplest stories often lie the deepest truths, truths that hold far-reaching implications for us as individuals and for our culture at large. I would like to share with you what I have learned.

Defining Characteristics of ADC

ADC often occurs in the context of grief. Most simply it is the phenomenon in which a survivor feels he or she has had contact with the deceased. This contact may be through dreams, in feeling a presence, or by an actual sensory experience such as seeing or hearing the deceased. The survivor might, for example, see the deceased doing some activity he or she had done while living.

Time and Frequency

ADC can happen at any time of the day or night. Though visitation dreams generally occur at night, people also have them while napping. One middle-aged widow saw her husband working in the garden early in the morning. A policeman was awakened by his dog in the middle of the night to the strong scent of his wife's perfume. In the afternoon, while a student was taking a final exam, she heard a dead classmate reassuringly say her name. Another young woman had several experiences feeling her brother's presence very late at night, one awakening her from sleep. Sue said wryly, "He doesn't have to keep a schedule anymore."

Although experiences can occur anytime in a person's life, most occur soon after the death, helping survivors think differently about death and even about the grief they are experiencing. This timing usually provides immediate comfort to the bereaved.

Alice's story illustrates how ADC can help facilitate grief and help us move on.

ALICE

Alice and Gregg had been married for three years. They had tried to have a baby for a little over a year, and were just beginning to go through a fertility workup when Alice became pregnant. The pregnancy went smoothly, and they were ecstatic when Molly was born. Alice described her as "a tender soul who commanded love."

Tragically, Molly had a blood disorder and never left the hospital. Alice and Gregg were heartsick. Gregg threw himself into his work, but Alice felt unable to return to her job right away and took time off from being a legal secretary to grieve.

Alice said, "I couldn't make sense of losing someone so young and so dear. I felt like a part of me had been ripped away. I wanted to be angry at this injustice, but there was a weight on my heart, so heavy, it kept me from having any emotion but sorrow. I seemed to be doing things in slow motion. Sometimes it felt like I was watching myself from outside my body. I'd go into Molly's room and sit, mostly too sad to cry. My mind would wander to trivial, practical things like 'My sister could use that little changing table; I could give the clothes to Erin, a friend who just had a little girl.' Then I would berate myself for being superficial and insensitive.

"Everything seemed meaningless. I didn't feel like eating, but I was not working and had too much time, so I prepared meals anyway. Besides, I wanted Gregg to eat. I had to take care of somebody.

"Three days after Molly died I was in the kitchen. It was a Thursday evening, and I was putting together something that was probably pretty inedible, but I was busy. There was no radio or TV on, and I don't exactly remember what I was thinking about. I just remember hearing this cooing, this sweet little sound. I stopped everything. I knew instantly it was Molly. I think my heart jumped a little. I heard it again, as plain as I've ever heard anybody. Then I felt an emotion I didn't think was even in me anymore. For that instant, I was happy. I knew she was letting me know she was with God. I'm not sure how I knew that, I just knew it.

"I still didn't understand why I couldn't have her, but I knew she was all right. I think from that point on,

I started grieving and dealing with the loss. I still felt awful, but if that hadn't happened, I'm not sure what I would have done."

Alice concluded, "After hearing her little voice, I felt better equipped to deal with Molly's death. I wanted to make sense of it, in a spiritual way. I wanted to be able to be happy again."

No matter when ADC occurs, it has the potential to help survivors resolve grief. In Alice's case it came very soon after Molly's death, helping Alice move through her grief. Before that time her world made no sense. Things were not happening in the natural order. Children are not supposed to die before their parents do. Believing that Molly was spiritually alive helped Alice feel alive again. She had a new way of relating to her loss. Her world was not empty, just changed. Now she had enough emotional stamina to go through the pain of grieving. She was more optimistic that she could be happy again. It is this sense of a force greater than ourselves at work in the universe that often restores and gives hope and meaning to the bereaved. These visitations can be a most welcome gift. It is ironic that such a time of great sorrow can also be filled with a sense of awe and wonder.

DOMINIQUE

Her mother appeared to Dominique for the first time two years after she died. It was Christmas Day, and Dominique had been preparing a feast for a small group of close friends. Because she was running behind schedule, she kept glancing out the front window in anticipation of her guests. No sooner had she placed a cherry pie in the oven (her mother's favorite), when she saw her first guest at the door. Wiping her hands, Dominique crossed the living room. But before she even reached the front door, she had the strangest sensation that this was no ordinary guest. Remarkably, she felt herself leave her own body to go and greet her mother, who had come with a Christmas message of peace. At last Dominique knew that her mother had found peace, and so too had Dominique. In that instant Dominique knew she had accepted her mother's death. It was now time to go on with her life.

Like Dominique's experience, most ADCs are brief, lasting from a few seconds to a few minutes. Many ADCs involve a smell, a word or two, or a fleeting sense of presence, but some people do have extended visits with departed loved ones.

BRETT

Brett, a young executive who was troubled by a problem at work, had an extended conversation with his uncle, who had been a lawyer. Brett had always valued his uncle's ability to make good judgments, and he wanted his guidance on how to handle a situation. He said, "I sat in my den, wondering, What would Uncle Hal do? I started having this mental conversation with him. After I began talking to him, I felt like he was there. He was talking to me from inside my head. It was really him."

Brett described to his uncle how he had observed a coworker engaging in what he considered unethical behavior. "Our talk went on for some time, at least thirty minutes."

At the end of the conversation he knew that he needed to confront his coworker himself and felt quite relieved to have come to a decision. Bolstered by his uncle's support, Brett confronted his coworker with courage and conviction. Had his uncle not contacted him, Brett doubted he would have been so resolved in his decision.

In my research it was becoming clear that contact of any length could alter our actions in this world. In the case of Brett, his uncle helped him resolve an important ethical decision, but contact can impact "smaller" decisions too.

One woman in her thirties felt her mother's presence all day while she shopped for antiques, which was something she and her mother used to do frequently on Saturdays. She said, "It was comforting; it made the day more fun. It was like we were together again. There she was by my side, with me in the different shops. I even felt her guiding me to buy a silver pin for my daughter's birthday present. When my daughter opened the box she said, 'Wow, this looks like something Nana would have.' I laughed to myself and thought, 'I hope your Nana goes Christmas shopping with me.' "

I also found that some people have multiple experiences, lasting years.

RACHAEL

Rachael was just an infant when her mother died. She was raised in a loving home by her grandmother and remembers a happy childhood, full of family and friends. Rachael said, "From growing up with Grams, in that environment, I knew at a young age that I wanted a family, too. So the year after I got married, I became pregnant. It was also the year Grams died. I'd been looking forward to showing off all I'd learned about being a good mom from her. I wanted her to be proud of me."

Two years later, Rachael did get a chance to show off her parenting. "I was helping my daughter Michelle with some finger paints when I felt this light squeeze on my shoulder. Grams used to give me a gentle squeeze like that. I knew it was her. It felt really great; she was still with me. It was like I was connected to generations of my family." Rachael went on to explain that "Every so often, maybe, a few times a year, I feel that same little squeeze. This has been going on for five years! Grams is letting me know, 'You're doing a good job.' You know, I was raised believing that our loved ones' spirits can help us, but this is really something. I hope I can do it for my family after I die."

A common thread running throughout these experiences was a sense of comfort. This comfort comes from the realization that love extends beyond the confines of our physical bodies. It comes from knowing that the essence or spirit of our loved ones does not die. And it comes from knowing that the universe holds eternal mysteries for both our loved ones and us.

Importance of Relationship between Living and Deceased

It is not clear why some people have these extraordinary experiences and some do not, but a close relationship to the deceased seems to help. Though all described close relationships, the living did not always idealize the deceased. They all described him or her as a complex human being, possessing both positive and negative characteristics.

SALLY

Sally and Ben had been married for three years when Ben was diagnosed with terminal cancer. The news came when they were both in their late twenties. Sally said, "It seemed so unfair, here we were, two young people with dreams of a whole life together. We had a lot to offer the world. And, you know, we were better as a couple than we were as individuals. We were so close."

When Sally described Ben she said, "He was a wonderful man. He was so good to me. He was a little jealous though. He wanted to own me body, heart, and soul. Sometimes we would fight over that. His jealousy could be a little too much, but most of the time it was okay, because he was so good to me in other ways. It was worth it. There's always something you have to put up with."

Ben lived for two years beyond his initial diagnosis. Sally said that they made the most of that time together.

They talked openly and cried together over the loss. About a week after the funeral, Sally was sitting at home, reminiscing and going through an old scrapbook. As she did, she felt Ben's presence beside her. It was like a very light swirling of air that was neither warm nor cool, but a subtle disruption of the stillness beside her.

Though there was nothing physical to indicate that Ben was near, Sally intuitively knew it was him. She put out her hand to see if she could feel him more distinctly. She couldn't, but at the same time she also had the sense that they were communicating. Ben was letting her know that he was all right. The feeling lasted only a minute or two. Sally said that though this event happened years ago, it was one of those moments that felt timeless while it was happening, and the experience remains clear in her memory.

Sally also said, "I know he died knowing without question that I loved him and that he loved me. We said those things every day. There was nothing left unsaid, undone. I cannot think of anything that I would have done differently with our relationship, and his coming back like that confirmed it."

But not all close relationships were as easy. Some were conflicted.

ALECIA

Alecia was thirty-two when she met Mark. She was working as a paralegal. Mark was a welder and a motorcycle enthusiast who did not even own a car. He was carefree and fun-loving. Alecia saw another side of life with him. She said, "Mark was really different than anyone I had dated before; and he was certainly different than my ex-husband. Roger called me irresponsible when I went over fifty-five miles an hour."

As they spent more time together, Alecia and Mark began to see that their values were very different. The relationship became tumultuous, with frequent fighting. Many times they threatened to break up. Nevertheless, Alecia said that they were very close and loved each other intensely.

Alecia was devastated when Mark died instantly after hitting a tree on a rainy night. Several weeks after the funeral while working at home she heard his laughter. Alecia said, "Damn, that was just like him! He would come back and let me know he's having more fun than I am, even after he's dead."

State of Mind

Most who have had ADC believe that certain states of consciousness are more conducive to it than others, and researchers have noted this too. Some people believe that being in a state of quiet is the only way to experience the deceased. Others said that because they were so exhausted physically and emotionally by the grief, their defenses were down; thus they were in a receptive state to experience the deceased.

KAREN

Karen and Gene had been married for seven years. From his first marriage Gene had two children who lived with his ex-wife most of the time. Karen had no children, so she and Gene had lots of free time for just the two of them. Karen and Gene so enjoyed each other that they had started planning for early retirement to be able to travel while they were still young. Unfortunately, Gene contracted hepatitis and died before his forty-seventh birthday.

Karen said that Gene's death was something she had no way to prepare for. He had been healthy and energetic. She said, "It was total disbelief. Healthy people his age don't just catch things and die." Karen taught fifth grade and had a good support system at work. She also had a sister in a nearby city who called and looked in on her. Karen said, "I almost didn't need anybody's help because this could not be happening. I didn't want to believe it. No, it was more than that; I couldn't believe it."

A few days after the funeral, Karen was getting ready to go back to teaching. She was on automatic, just numbly going through the motions. She said, "All of a sudden, one of my schoolbooks fell off the table, a geography book. It opened to Spain. Gene and I had been talking about going to Spain. It was amazing. I probably would have brushed that off as a coincidence, but at the same time, I felt Gene's presence in the room. This was no coincidence. All at once it was funny, sad, and wonderful. This was the first time I'd felt him with me in days, but this time he was dead."

Karen continued, "I do believe that when we're in shock or when we're in a very emotional state, our bodies are a lot more sensitive and open to things that we don't allow ourselves to be open to at other times." She explained that she is quite analytical and that she doubted she would have had the experience if she were thinking and behaving as she normally did.

Others believe that one only needs to be receptive to the idea of ADC to be capable of experiencing it.

GEORGIA

Georgia, an accountant in her late forties, lost her sister to emphysema. Darci was ten years older, and though she was not always living at home while Georgia was growing up, the sisters were close. Darci took on a bit of the mothering role, sometimes against Georgia's protests. In adulthood they were good friends. After Darci died, Georgia felt like she had lost both a sister and a nurturing figure.

It had been about a week after the funeral, and Georgia was still having crying spells whenever she thought about the loss of her sister. One afternoon, walking down the long driveway to the mailbox, she found more than she expected. "Darci was standing right there. It was like she was going to pick up the mail for me. It was a very hazy image but I knew it was her. I think she was looking in on me."

Georgia went on to say, "I always believed in an afterlife, and I do believe there can be communication between the living and the dead." She also pointed out that she had never spent much time thinking about it and never dabbled in the occult or with the supernatural.

However, having a receptive mind-set alone does not guarantee an experience for everyone. Some people who want to have experiences do not have them, and others have them, unexpectedly. In most cases the experience is initiated by the deceased. One woman says about her experience of suddenly seeing her grandmother in the doorway: "I was her beloved grandchild; I had the feeling she came to me because she wanted to reassure herself or see that everything was fine. I didn't actually summon her out of my own need; she actually manifested herself because she wanted to."

Most people deny even attempting to elicit an experience. One young woman described hearing her mother call her by her nickname as she was getting ready to go out with her boyfriend. It is quite typical, then, to be engaged in an activity, not even thinking about the deceased, when the experience occurs.

People who try to contact the deceased are generally unsuccessful. Some people in my studies actively sought to have another encounter by wishing for it or by attempting to duplicate the circumstances of the experience (e.g., setting or frame of mind).

VIKI

Viki was walking in a small, wooded park near her home shortly after her mother died. She stopped on a small bluff to look at a cardinal in a cypress tree when suddenly she felt surrounded by the smell of her mother's perfume. She said the experience was wonderful, and she wanted to have another one: "I tried to reproduce it. I probably spent more time in that park that week than I had all year. I tried everything: standing in the same spot at the same time of day, in different spots at the same time of day, and then in different spots at different times of day. It got a little ridiculous. I even looked for that stupid bird again. I was driven. No matter what combination I tried, it didn't work. I smelled Mom's perfume only that one time. At least getting nuts as I did got me out of the house."

Laura, on the other hand, is able to contact her grandmother when she wants to and has ongoing conversations with her.

LAURA

"Sometimes I would just sense her there. Mostly I would ask for her. I think that pretty much, unless they have a message they want to give you, you pretty much have to ask for them. Sometimes they have a real important message, and then they come to you, but they're not constantly in communication unless there's a reason." When asked why she was able to contact her grandmother while most other people could not, she said: "I think it's because I don't think of people as their physical body. I think of people as their essence—their spirit. When people are real attached to the physical presence, they can't re-create that—they can't get that back. You need to call on just the spiritual—the loving feeling of the person—just the same as if they're not dead. When you're sitting there thinking they died, and you're sad and wondering and waiting and worrying they're not all right, then you block it. It's not that you're not trying; it's just that you don't know how to see it, you don't know how to receive it. You're looking for a smell or a cool breeze or a sign of something, instead of getting inside the essence of the person. Because anybody can contact the essence of somebody else by just getting in touch with how you felt when you were with them before, instead of thinking that something about them has been lost. Nothing about them has been lost. Everything that's real is exactly the same."

Communication

Communication is at the heart of ADC. It's what makes people feel as if they have reconnected with the deceased. Communication during ADC is not limited to the traditional verbal and nonverbal styles with which we are so familiar. It is often of a telepathic nature.

Not long after losing her son, Carol heard him talking to her very distinctly. His words seemed to be resonating through the back of her brain. She automatically responded aloud to him because his communication had been so vivid.

Some conversations involve both the living and the deceased communicating telepathically. Peter explained that during his experience with his grandfather neither of them had to open their mouths: "I was just talking to him and asking him, 'What are you doing here? What's going on?' Then I said to him, 'I was wondering if you would know what I was doing now that you're dead.' Then I realized I was talking to him, but I wasn't talking with my mouth. I was just thinking these things, but he could understand what I was thinking. And I could understand what he was thinking. It was a very efficient form of communication."

"I'm All Right"

Most people received messages that the deceased is all right. Like all messages, these communications can be explicitly stated, inferred, or intuited from the experience and seem to fall into two categories related to spiritual and physical peace of the deceased. Survivors have said such things as, "He wanted to say it's okay, and he's where he's supposed to be" or "He wanted to let me know that he was a Christian." The deceased seem to be describing a state of spiritual calm. Other survivors received messages indicating that the deceased was at physical peace because of comments such as, "I was happy to see that peaceful face after he had been in such excruciating pain." The survivor has a sense of the absence or ending of pain that the deceased experienced before dying.

"You'll Be All Right, Too"

Most participants in my research said that after they received comforting messages from the deceased, they knew that they would be all right, too. One woman said, "My husband let me know that he was going to look after me. I was so grief stricken that night I think he came back to comfort me. Another woman said, "My father wanted to let me know that he was there, that he didn't abandon me."

When people receive comforting messages, they feel better equipped to get through their grief. They also believe that the deceased is there to help them. And many said they also sensed that the deceased was there to let go of physical life on earth and to say goodbye before moving on.

Messages of Advice and Support and Guidance

The deceased often offer advice or support. A middle-aged accountant frequently experienced his father's presence when golfing and received advice on his game. A young mother of four would hear her aunt, who had raised her, give her advice on raising her children. The deceased also issue warnings.

JUDY

Judy, who had vivid dreams of her husband, Henry, and whose case will be discussed in detail in chapter 3, felt him trying to warn her to take another road because a bridge had been washed out on the usual route: "Where I had to go was literally in the middle of two bridges. I heard the voice say to me, 'Go on south and come back a few blocks because the bridge is out.' I thought, that's ridiculous. There's no reason for this. The bridge can't possibly be out. I got off at the north exit, and the bridge was out. I never experienced anything like this before my husband died."

Rose felt more support from her mother after her mother died than when her mother was alive. Her mother now gives her advice, and their relationship has healed through frequent contact between them: "She gives me advice. You know, it's not really enlightened advice; it's things that she would have told me when she was alive. She's a mother figure, she's a friend, but it's like she's giving me guidance and support."

JOANNA

Joanna described a most unusual visitation. Following an extensive infertility workup, Joanna decided to escape to a Boston park. She sat under a large shade tree and watched a group of children playing on the monkey bars in the distance. Off to the side she saw an old woman, who at first glance looked like one of their grandmothers. She looked out of place in her meticulously fashioned curls and her dated frock. The children seemed oblivious to her odd attire as they swung and laughed on the bars.

Joanna looked away for several seconds and when she returned her gaze to the monkey bars, the woman had vanished. Suddenly she knew why. As impossible as it seemed, the old woman was standing next to her. There was something familiar about her. Yet Joanna knew she'd never seen her in this park before.

"This is my tree," the woman said possessively. When Joanna asked her why, the woman replied, "Because I planted it."

Knowing this was improbable, Joanna began to protest. "That's silly," Joanna blurted out. But before she could continue, the strange old woman had vanished, leaving Joanna with a wonderful feeling of comfort. Then she realized why.

The woman bore an eerie resemblance to a picture Joanna had seen of her grandmother, who had died before she was born. "In fact she was a dead ringer," Joanna laughed. "Because it was my grandmother."

But why would her grandmother, whom Joanna had always considered a woman of great gentleness and wisdom, appear to her in such a confrontational way? Joanna knew her grandmother had come with a message of hope. Her grandmother had come to illustrate how silly it was to think you could really own a living thing simply because you planted the seed. The tree was there for everyone to enjoy. And yet this had been Joanna's line of thinking before her grandmother had appeared. Watching the children playing, Joanna had fallen into a state of despair over her infertility.

Now Joanna knew for all the old woman's apparent rudeness, she had demonstrated the wisdom she believed her grandmother to have. For this woman pointed out how wrong Joanna had been in thinking she would never enjoy the laughter of children. The world was full of children to enjoy, whether they were biologically hers or not.

Joanna says because of this message from another world she and her husband went on to adopt the most beautiful little girls in the world. And every year she and her daughters plant a seedling in memory of her grandmother for all to enjoy.

Though communication is usually brief and simple, it can sometimes be complicated and ongoing. When it is extended, it often not only leads to grief's resolution but also helps heal the relationship between the living and the deceased. The therapeutic nature of ADC is discussed in detail in chapter 8.

Departures

When the experience ends, the deceased's departures vary from the gradual to the abrupt. Some departures faded slowly—a lingering perfume, a wispy light fading into the darkness, or a whispering voice growing softer. Other departures were utterly jarring in their abruptness—one moment a seemingly solid form is there, and the next moment it's gone. What struck me most about accounts of departures was, despite their surreal qualities, participants were absolute in their convictions that the experience was not imagined. Although the phenomenon was completely outside the realm of "normal" experience, each participant knew in his or her heart that something extraordinarily real had occurred. A loved one had reached out to him or her from another dimension.

ROBIN

Robin's sister, Beth, died at thirty-eight, after a long illness. She had multiple medical problems, including a compromised immune system, and spent a lot of time in bed. Although Robin lived two hours away, she visited Beth frequently before she died. She and her sister talked, watched TV, and made each other laugh. But underneath it all, each possessed a profound sense of sadness. They knew they would miss each other terribly when they were separated. One evening they talked about Beth's death, about life after death, and how they would be spiritually connected after Beth was gone. During the conversation, Robin kept her doubts to herself.

One morning after Beth died, while she sorted through documents on Beth's desk, Robin caught a glimmering light out of the side of her eye. She turned her head and saw a clear image of her sister standing in the doorway.

"There she was, as solid as you or me," Robin said. "It was really unbelievable. She was standing in the doorway looking healthy and happy. Her beautiful blue eyes had no trace of pain in them. Then, as quickly as she had appeared, she was gone. In the blink of an eye. It was just like somebody had handed me a picture to look at and then took it back. Just like that, gone. But I know it was real. I'm positive of that."

PATTI

Patti's experience of her father's departure was a bit different.

She had been severely grief stricken by her father's death and spent many nights crying herself to sleep. One evening right after she had gotten into bed, she saw her father. "I was fluffing my pillow and looked up and saw Dad. He was in front of the bed, about six feet in front of me. He was see-through, but with color. In fact, the color was quite clear, with very distinct margins. I saw his face and he looked healthy. He wasn't jaundiced any more; he was rosier. Dad stayed for a couple minutes. I sat still, transfixed, afraid that if I moved he would go away. As I stared, afraid to blink, his form began fading until it just disappeared. It was almost like watching a fog clear on a cloudy day. And even though he wasn't solid, I knew he was real. Even after he'd left, I could feel his presence all around me."

Though most people did not want the deceased to leave, the departures were accepted as part of the experience whether they were abrupt or gradual. No type of departure made the phenomenon less real. In fact, when the bereaved stated emphatically that they knew the experience was real, they often explained it as a deep sense of knowing. It was not simply because they saw, smelled, heard, or felt the deceased. They experienced a different kind of knowing. Deep in the core of their being, they knew the phenomenon to be true, but they couldn't explain it, almost as if it were a sixth sense, a sense not yet identified. From the most solid forms to the most ephemeral presence, this unusual sense of knowing persisted in each person I spoke to.

Two

Waking Encounters

A Different Way of Knowing

Typically one would say that seeing, hearing, smelling, or feeling the touch of a dead person is a hallucination, since this sensory experience does not have an identifiable external stimulus. Currently, in the fourth edition of the *Diagnostic and Statistical Manual (DSM IV)*, the American Psychiatric Association specifies that the criteria for diagnosing uncomplicated bereavement may include hallucinatory experiences where the individual thinks that "he or she hears the voice of, or transiently sees the image of, the deceased person."

However, I believe that because hallucinations are so poorly understood, we have no way of differentiating them from paranormal phenomena, which may indeed have an external stimulus that is simply outside the realm of our limited senses. The fact is, if hallucinations are the mark of mental illness, most of us are ill.

As Dr. Ian Stevenson noted: "Many members of the general population seem to have had one or several memorable hallucinatory experiences." In 1983 in the *American Journal of Psychiatry,* Stevenson recommended a careful examination of the different types of hallucinations, noting that many people will not discuss their experiences because of the disapproval associated with hallucinations. He stated that the word *hallucination* has become so synonymous with the concept of psychosis that a new word needs to be used to describe a variety of unshared sensory experiences.

Defining ADCs as hallucinations is troublesome because the word hallucination is considered pejorative, and it may compel many individuals to hide or even discount their sensory experiences with the deceased for fear of being labeled abnormal. One such participant, a well-respected lawyer, told me he was reluctant to share his experiences because he feared it would damage his professional credibility. Another simply told me, "I don't want people to think I'm nuts. It sounds like I'm hallucinating, but I know it's real."

Even those studying hallucinations say hallucinations themselves are poorly understood. In the *Canadian Journal of Psychiatry,* Dr. C. Andrade and colleagues point out that tradition, rather than knowledge, influences clinical decisions related to hallucinations. They acknowledge that hallucinations occur in nonpsychotic states, including grief, and should be evaluated in relationship to the overall clinical picture, rather than judged to be merely indicative of psychosis.

Regardless of what we label ADCs, experiencing the deceased may be a phenomenon that has not yet been identified, a little understood paranormal event that puts us in touch with another dimension. As our understanding of physics grows, we see that our universe is nothing like we imagined. Its very strangeness, with its time warps, black holes, and mathematical inconsistencies, has captured the imagination of scientists and science fiction enthusiasts alike. Nothing is as it seems. Keeping an open mind appears to be the most sensible course. I believe as our understanding of this complex phenomenon increases, the criteria will also change to encompass a different way of knowing or sixth sense.

Although ADC falls outside what many people consider objective reality, it is real for those who experience such contact. They are actively engaged in it with their whole being. It is not the same as passively watching TV. They recognize it to be real on a visceral level, and by destigmatizing the phenomenon of experiencing the deceased, we stand to gain a wealth of knowledge that would otherwise be lost to us forever.

Experiencing the Deceased through the Senses

Many of my research participants experienced the deceased through all the senses except taste, and sometimes they experienced the deceased through more than one sense.

Those who experience the deceased through smell report either smelling the deceased's personal scent or one closely associated with the deceased. A mother, Lynn, and daughter, Terri, had experiences with the sense of smell but at different times and of different people.

Lynn reported that approximately three weeks after her mother's funeral she was at home and smelled the scent of the flowers that had surrounded the casket in the funeral chapel. She accepted this matter-of-factly, convinced it was her mother.

Terri also experienced a loved one through the sense of smell. She went to answer the telephone but found no one on the line. Instead she smelled the strong scent of her grandfather mixed with his favorite cologne, Old Spice, coming through the receiver. She does not remember if the telephone actually rang or if she just knew to pick it up. Initially she thought the experience was "a little weird," but she had no doubt it was her grandfather, and she said it gave her a strong sense of comfort and happiness.

LIZZY

Lizzy's experience also dramatically illustrates perceiving through the sense of smell. One cool autumn afternoon at her family's summer cottage, Lizzy, a twenty-eight-year-old social worker, sat on the front porch swing overlooking the lake. She remembered this swing fondly as a spot where she and her grandfather would spend lazy summer evenings talking about the world, especially their mutual love for fishing. She loved her talks with her grandfather because he never spoke down to her like so many other adults.

But today at the lake, Lizzy was utterly alone and enjoying it. Everyone had left earlier that morning, and she had volunteered to complete the remaining few chores needed to close up the cottage for the winter. As she sat dreamily gazing at the lake and the bright autumn foliage, a strong smell of pipe tobacco permeated the air. It was unmistakably her grandfather's brand, with a deep fruity smell she'd come to love. Lizzy looked around for the intruder. Perhaps a distant neighbor had happened by to say a few parting words before the season's end. She circled the house but the smell faded as she moved farther from the porch. She walked from the backyard through the house, but there was no smell. Puzzled, she sat back down on the swing.

The air smelled crisp and clear, and it held no trace of the pungent tobacco odor that was so overpowering just moments before. She thought she might have imagined it, but as she sat there, the smell returned. It grew in intensity until it completely enveloped her on the swing. There was no mistaking it. It wasn't just her grandfather's tobacco smoke; it was her grandfather. Lizzy said that she was completely surrounded by this awesome sense of his presence, and tears filled her eyes. Suddenly she felt this strange calm, as if her grandfather didn't want her to be afraid.

"It was like I was being completely held in this smoke I couldn't see. But the weirdest part is that I knew his presence was all wrapped up in my closing the house and in our family being separated for a time. It was if my grandfather was telling me that like the family getting back together again next summer, he, too, would return. It made me think of how joyous our reunions are at the cottage every spring. Amazing—that's what my grandfather told me in a puff of smoke I couldn't even see."

GAIL

In this bittersweet story, Gail, a restaurant owner in her late thirties, also spoke of experiencing the deceased through the sense of smell. As she explained:

"My mother had had an autoimmune disease that literally ate up her lung. At first she had a hard time breathing, so she had surgery and had that lung removed. They put her on Prednisone, and she did fine for maybe six to eight months; then she started going down again. Then we discovered that it was in the opposite lung. She was placed on oxygen; she became more and more dependent.

"I would wash clothes, cook dinner, take her to the doctor. I would help my father out, too, because I knew she would appreciate that. When I couldn't do anything else, I would just lie there with her. Sometimes that was all I could do."

She said that she and her mother were very close, and when her mother died, Gail was heartbroken. She said, "I couldn't say that I was relieved by her death, but I was glad that it was over for her; she suffered so much."

Then within the same month of her death, Gail experienced her mother through smell. She said:

"I was asleep in bed when this odor awakened me. It was her! I didn't see anything; nothing strange was going on. I would have loved to see her, but there was just this odor. It was her own personal distinct smell. It was a little bit the smell of the illness. I kept smelling it even though now I was wide awake. I smelled it just as if she were right next to me. I wasn't expecting it at all. I wasn't even thinking about her.

"I was not afraid; I wanted more. I really wanted to see her. This was so different than anything else I had ever experienced. I felt so close to her. It was so reassuring. But just as fast as it came, it left. I've never experienced that since."

In all the stories people shared with me about experiencing the deceased through the sense of smell, none questioned the authenticity of the experience. The certainty with which each person described the meaning of the experience struck me. It was as if they were experiencing a profound truth through a different way of knowing. They often remarked on how odd it was, but they held steadfast in their conviction that the experience was real. The sense of smell can trigger memories of people or places. These were not simple memories being triggered, however. These were new communications accompanied by the presence of an inexplicable familiar smell of a loved one. The sense of smell triggered a powerful idea and along with it a message of hope to the spirit. It says to me that all the senses open doors to realms we simply don't yet understand.

Of course one of the most celebrated ways to experience the deceased is through the sense of sight. This is the stuff that countless ghost stories and myths are made of.

However, I found that the bereaved see the deceased in a wide variety of ways. These experiences can share great similarities with the popularized versions of wispy, ethereal forms in the night, or they can vary dramatically.

Many people report seeing the deceased as a living person (no different from any other living person) or as a spiritual entity (transparent and/or not in a physical body). Sometimes the dead person is seen with another dead human or animal. People could also see the deceased in other forms. One woman lost her son after he sustained a closed head injury in a motorcycle accident. He had wanted to be an organ donor. At one point during her ordeal in the hospital, when she knew her son's spirit was gone from his body, she saw elements of him in those around her. She passionately described seeing his essence in another young man's eyes. Still there are others who experience their vision of the deceased as living beings.

CLARE

Clare saw, felt, and heard her deceased husband.

"It's strange, but I almost feel like my husband died when he did because I was asleep. We slept in separate rooms; I was in the front bedroom, and he was in the middle bedroom because he was real restless at night. I wasn't, and he was afraid he'd keep me awake too much. That morning I heard him get up, which I always did. It was cool, and he got on his clothes; he went outside, got the paper, put Poochie out, and then he came back in here and turned on the gas log. I heard him start to look at the paper, and then the next thing I heard from him was snoring. So I went back to sleep after I knew he was inside.

"Then I heard him holler, 'Oh.' At first I thought I had dreamed the sound, and then he hollered again. I sat up in bed; I knew it was really him. I jumped up and ran in the living room but he was already out. I couldn't get him back. I called a neighbor for help, and he called the rescue squad.

"When the rescue people arrived, they took my husband right to the hospital. They put him on a respirator, you know, one of those breathing machines. Those things are horrible. My husband had always made me promise him that I wouldn't let them keep him alive if his brain was damaged; he didn't want that. I told this to his doctor and asked him to please take him off the machines. They ran three brain tests. Every one of them showed no activity in the brain."

Clare went on to explain her husband stayed in the ICU a total of fourteen days and was finally moved to a regular room on a Friday afternoon. There was no hope for his recovery.

"They took away all the machines except oxygen, which I was glad for because the oxygen made it easier for him.

"I would only go home at night because the doctor insisted. He was afraid if I didn't take care of myself I would get sick.

"My husband passed away Saturday at three o'clock in the afternoon. It was a blessing to be with him when he died. I had asked the Lord to have His will. It was more of a relief than a sorrow. I was ready to let him go. Because I knew that he wouldn't have wanted this, I didn't want it for him.

"At night I would help my mother get ready for bed; she was staying with me. On this particular night a few months after her husband's death, it was around eleven o'clock, and she was in bed and had gotten quiet. I had been in bed myself about thirty minutes, and my husband just appeared at the side of the bed. He was in his usual undershorts and a T-shirt. He looked so real, no different than you or me. He looked just like he used to; there was no difference.

"Well, he was in his shorts and that shirt, sat down on the bed next to me, and started laughing. I said 'Honey, you better not laugh like that. You'll wake Mama up and disturb her.' Then I noticed he had Poochie, the dog, with him. Poochie had died about a month before all this. My husband said, 'Come on up here Poochie, jump up on the bed with us.' Well he did. Then my husband got to laughing, and he hugged me and kissed me. He said, 'I want you to know that I love you.' And I said, 'Well, I love you too, honey, and I sure miss you.' It was just like he was living, and I told him again, 'You're making too much noise, you're gonna wake Mamma.' And he said, 'Nobody can hear me but you. Not another soul knows I'm here but you. And then he and Poochie disappeared."

In Clare's case, she perceived her husband as solid matter. Marianne's perceptions were altogether different, and

they more closely mirror the myths surrounding appari-
tions.

MARIANNE

Billy's death had come as a complete surprise. On a
wintry morning, Marianne, a forty-four-year-old sub-
stitute teacher, received a phone call from the local
emergency room telling her that Billy, her ten-year-old
son, had been in a serious hit-and-run accident. When
she arrived at the hospital, Billy was dead. Marianne
couldn't bear to leave his small body. Instead she took a
washcloth and cleaned his face. Then she took a hair-
brush from her purse and brushed his hair. As soon as
she completed brushing his hair and put the brush back
in her purse, she saw a wispy form actually leaving her
son's still body.

"He waited until I was done, and then this white
wisp of a thing just floated out of his body. It was his little spirit. The whole room felt different. Then he rose
up above me and dissipated just like steam. I know it
was him saying goodbye to his mama."

Marianne never saw this form again. She said that instead
of being frightened, she was consoled seeing Billy rise up to
heaven. She believes her son never returned because his work
here on earth was done.

Others I interviewed perceived the deceased through feel.
Again this experience varied greatly. The touch could range

from a light, feathery touch to a firm, solid touch. Some commented that the deceased didn't feel fully materialized, while others said he or she felt perfectly solid and fully alive.

Surprisingly, almost no one felt fear. An instant sense of knowing the touch to be that of a returning loved one imparted a feeling of safety and comfort to the bereaved. As one man put it, "Her touch made me relax right away."

Deborah also perceived a departed loved one through the sense of feel, though her experience was more unusual.

DEBORAH

Deborah, a nurse in her early fifties, was the first person I formally interviewed. She was a student of mine who wanted to help others understand ADC. She told me about her husband: She had known him for eight years, and they'd been married for four. She remembered him this way: "He was the most interesting man I've ever known. He was very, very good to me and an awful lot of fun. He got sick with heart disease, had a heart attack, and then had a slight stroke. It took about two years for him to recover. During that time things were tough for us. He wasn't himself anymore. It seemed like half the time I was crying, and the other half I was consoling him and trying to keep him afloat mentally. I remember one time saying to him, 'I miss the old you.'

"Then he started to recover. He repeatedly thanked me for staying with him and going through the physical ordeal with him. Even though he was better, in some ways he was deteriorating. Right after we had returned from a trip, he died.

"The next morning I picked out a marvelous casket, and I told my son and daughter-in-law that I would be going home. They tried to persuade me to stay, but I said, 'No, I've got to get used to living by myself.' That evening, not too long after I was in bed, I felt like someone was underneath the bed, kicking with their feet in the rhythm of a heartbeat. I never watch scary movies because I'm easily frightened, but that night I wasn't scared. The kicking did not scare me. The bed was even moving in the rhythm of a heartbeat. This feeling lasted maybe a minute. Then the movement stopped, and I lay down again feeling very excited. This was not my imagination. No one could ever convince me that the experience wasn't real. I thought how wonderful for my husband to have let me know him in this way. I knew it was him, and I wanted the experience to happen again but it never did."

ANITA

Anita also experienced contact through touch. As she lay in bed, agonizing about a difficult decision she needed to make at work, she felt a presence. She explained that she felt this presence in the same way people feel someone standing behind them looking over their shoulder. You feel their energy. Alarmed, she swung her head around to see who was standing next to the bed. She thought it might be one of her boys. But instead she found herself staring directly into her deceased mother's gentle eyes. Rather than fear, Anita immediately felt safe.

"It was the strangest feeling because I would have thought I'd be scared to death. I wasn't. It was comforting. My mom was wearing the yellow linen she bought on our last shopping trip together. She bought it for a cruise we went on together. When I saw that dress I immediately knew she was telling me to lighten up and stop worrying about work so much, to have more fun.

"As soon as I got this message, she started to fade out. And then the most amazing thing happened! I felt her hug me. Her body wasn't there but I felt a real hug. It was gentle and reassuring. You know, as if to say, 'Honey, it's going to be okay.' "

Once again, I was struck by the similar theme, regardless of which sense the deceased is perceived through. Anita, like so many of the bereaved, was given a message that everything was fine. So often in speaking to people about this message, they describe it as an instant sense of knowing. They just knew everything would be fine. And often they knew this with no words ever being spoken. It's as if they receive the message telepathically in a feeling, and this feeling speaks to them more clearly and powerfully than words ever could.

People also report hearing the deceased speak either single words or complete sentences. Some report hearing laughter. One woman heard her husband laugh jovially and then say, "I'm looking out for you." Some individuals report having a dialogue with the deceased that was similar to a conversation that took place with the deceased before death. Sometimes the individual would question the deceased, asking, for example, Will I see you again? But the overriding message is a positive one, often filled with hope. Randy's is such a story.

RANDY

Randy is a brilliant astrophysicist in his fifties. The inconsistencies and limitations of how we construct our worldview come up often in my conversations with him. In fact, physics has made Randy more of a mystic than a scientist. At every turn he's faced with the wonder of the universe and with the truth that we are light-years from grasping reality, if that's even possible. For all his scientifically based education, Randy remains remarkably open-minded, which may be why he felt so at ease when his deceased father paid him a most unexpected visit.

Hours after his father's funeral, Randy sat in his father's ocean condominium stunned and numb. He felt a profound sense of loss surrounded by all the familiar reminders of this man he loved so dearly: his father's favorite time-worn books, his maps from exotic trips he'd taken, and most of all his beautifully carved collection of shore birds. How his father had loved those birds. Randy began listening to their melodic sounds on an old record from the 1960s, scratches and all.

Later, as Randy sank deeper into a state of despair, he heard a faraway sound, ever so faint. He strained to listen. It was an unusual sound: unfamiliar, yet familiar at the same time. Then he recognized it. It was the beautiful song of a faraway shore bird. As Randy strained to hear, its pitch rose to a crystal clear trill that filled his head and the room with a joyous light. "I don't know how to explain it," he said. "Noise became light. And that light held an emotion. I was filled with such joy because I knew everything would be all right and that my father was happy."

Randy sat with this profound joy for several moments, still and at peace. And then, as if it were a gift from heaven, he heard his father's voice. It was clear and happy and it said, "The birds sound better here. No scratches." Randy's joy erupted into laughter. The universe was indeed a strange place, but it was also a loving place with a cosmic sense of humor.

Making sense of this experience years later, Randy says his father's visit had a remarkable healing effect on him. It made him stronger and more sure of himself in the world. "When people ask me whether I think it really happened, I say, 'Of course it really happened.' It was a thought that had the power to change me. That's real. If you ask me to define real, I would have to say 'reality is held in feelings and ideas in the same way it's held in an atom.' "

In my research I found that many people sense a presence when they experience the deceased. They have a feeling the deceased is near them, but they cannot actually see, hear, feel, or smell the deceased. It is a distinct feeling, similar to how one knows that a person is standing nearby in a darkened room, and it's usually comforting.

Sometimes people feel a presence that is accompanied by a light or fog or a change in temperature. They believe that the light, fog, or temperature change is not the representation of the dead person; rather, the person's spirit is present and accompanied by unusual physical circumstances. Sometimes people sense a presence on one occasion and experience the deceased through the senses or through dreams on another.

People compare this sensation to feeling that the dead person is around them or feeling that the deceased is briefly a part of them. One woman said, "For just an instant while I was making a decision about my son, I felt like I was my mother thinking. It wasn't that I was thinking the way she used to think; it was as if I were actually her thinking these thoughts going through my head, as if she was in my head. When I felt this, I knew she was with me."

A veterinary assistant explained the sense of presence this way: "You know how when you're near a wild, half-crazed animal, you pick up on its energy. There aren't any words, just feelings. So crazy energy makes you feel crazy. But when my brother came back, it was like being in this kind, soothing energy that had a calming effect on me. I wondered if he learned that somewhere the way I learned how to calm a frightened dog. It was the strangest thing to feel so calm around something that should have been so scary."

Carla's experience also illustrates how the bereaved may sense a presence. Carla felt her mother's presence inside her body.

CARLA

Carla, an only child who was also adopted, was forty when her mother died after suffering a heart attack. However, her mother's death was not totally unexpected, since she had had heart problems for the past several years and was at high risk. As Carla said, "Mom never took really good care of herself. She'd get all stressed out over money or whatever; she didn't know how to relax, and she was never able to keep her weight down. I knew her heart would get her. I just knew it."

When her mother died Carla's father had been dead for two years. She and her mother were very close. Though they were not blood relatives, Carla and her mother were always intuitively connected. When her mother was hospitalized, Carla went to the hospital to keep her company. Carla said, "This time it was different. Somehow when I saw her in the bed, I knew that she was not leaving. I sensed that she knew it, too. We didn't talk about it though, but there was this quiet sadness to our conversations that made me think we were both feeling the same thing." Carla's mother died after two days in the hospital. She was not with her mother when she died, but she accepted that. She actually thought that her mother preferred to die without her. She knew her mother was a private person and would think going this way would be easier for everyone.

Carla had gone through quite a bit of anticipatory grief for her mother after her father's death. She had no significant unresolved issues with her mother, so essentially she had to cope with the sadness of the physical loss.

Carla's mother used to play the piano. She remembers watching her mother's hands as she played. In her mind's eye Carla could see herself as a little girl standing by the piano and watching the keys move as her mother's hands moved up and down the keyboard. It was a very distinct and pleasant memory for her.

Carla first experienced her mother's presence during the year after her death. One day while she was working at her computer, Carla noticed that her hands felt different. As she became aware of an altered feeling, she also became aware that her hands felt like her mother's hands.

She said, "It was the most unusual thing. All of a sudden I noticed that my hands felt different, but not tingly or numb or cold or anything like that. They didn't feel like mine, but they were mine. It was physical, and it wasn't physical. As soon as I tuned in to it, I knew that my mother's presence was in my hands. It wasn't weird or scary; it was more bewilderment, like, what's going on?"

Carla believed she was getting some kind of guidance from her mother. She said, "This was so unusual, but so comforting at the same time. I told my closest friend about it because she's open-minded. I had to laugh when I was telling her because the analogy that came to me was if your cat said, 'I'm so glad to see you,' when you got home. You'd wonder what's going on here and at the same time you'd love it."

Carla's example of her cat speaking typifies how so many of the bereaved perceive the experience. It is remarkably strange on one level, yet on another level it makes perfect, immediate sense. In the following story, Ann also experienced her mother through a sense of presence. Her account illustrates how a sense of knowing can be so far outside the "normal" boundaries of human experience and yet seem perfectly normal to the bereaved.

ANN

Ann expected her mother's death. Sharon had been under hospice care for three months and had had metastatic cancer for several years before that, going in and out of remissions. Each time Sharon became ill the family gathered around her, knowing her death could come at any time.

When Sharon died, both Ann and her father were with her. Ann's brother joined the family as soon as he could. Ann had moments of intense sadness but knew that she would survive her grief and that her mother was close to God. Though she was not very religious, she felt like a spiritual person. The people working with her mother at the hospice had helped her refine and strengthen her spiritual beliefs, and Ann had the peace of knowing that there was a greater reality for her mother and herself than just what was happening physically.

For the first three years after Sharon's death, Ann had no postdeath experiences with her mother. Then one day Ann was at home cleaning up after a family dinner and felt her mother's presence. "I was just walking around the kitchen. I was thinking about dirty sinks and dishes, nothing even close to enlightened thought. I felt this unusual feeling over my right shoulder. It seemed to extend up, and in my mind's eye I saw deep into space. I didn't hear a voice or see a real vision, but I started feeling my mother's presence. It felt like it was coming from far away. The feeling of her presence was very comforting yet the message was, 'I'm going away now,' and somehow I knew it would be for a long time and at a great distance. I also knew that she was fine and that I was, too.

"It was strange because I never felt her presence before, and now she was giving me this message that she was going away. I think she might have been there for me since her death, but for whatever reason never manifested until that day; maybe I was too preoccupied with other things to notice. Her contact with me said, 'You're on your own now, and you're doing fine.' "

Sense of presence falls outside the range of the five senses, and the bereaved could sense a loved one in a myriad of ways. For example, the bereaved could sense the deceased in an animal, an inanimate object, or even within their own bodies. That these experiences made perfect sense to the bereaved was of great interest to me because these were rational people maintaining normal and healthy lives. The common thread throughout these experiences was that the deceased's essence or spirit existed beyond their physical bodies, and this essence could assume a variety of forms. Despite the bizarre forms that these spirits could take on, they were immediately recognizable to the bereaved. Rarely did the bereaved question who the presence was or its significance. Most had an immediate sense of belief.

Three

Dream Encounters

In doing my research, I found that dreams were a powerful vehicle for the living person to have contact with the deceased. Survivors describe these dreams as visitations.

I have found that these dreams are different than non-visitation dreams for several reasons. In visitation dreams, the interaction feels as real as the contact we have with other living people. The dreams tend to be vivid and uncomplicated so that the dreamers can easily remember the content after awakening, though they may not remember dialogue verbatim. Unlike nonvisitation dreams, time does not seem distorted or fragmented and occurs in a normal time frame. If the dreamers speak with the deceased for what feels like fifteen minutes, they say it also feels like fifteen when they later recall the dream. These dreams also tend to occur in a realistic or a simple setting—a living room, for example, or outdoors in natural surroundings. On occasion they occur against a dark black background where the dreamers see only the person they knew. Nothing chaotic happens, nor are there bizarre situations and unrecognizable people or places.

The dreams contain the elements of a simple, realistic interaction between the deceased and the living person. The interaction in the dream elicits the same type of emotion it would elicit from an interaction with the person if he or she were alive. For instance, if they are discussing a sad subject, the dreamer feels the appropriate sadness.

Eric, a small-business owner, noted that in his dream about his friend Brian, he was able to be introspective while talking, something that does not normally occur in his dreams. Some people felt physical sensations during the dreams such as a hug or a kiss. For example, while she was sleeping, Melissa felt her sister touch her arm.

Although these dreams always affirm that the loved one's spirit is alive, they can serve other purposes as well. The following cases show the breadth of visitation dreams. (Judy, who is described below, also had two vivid nonvisitation dreams of her husband, and they are also discussed for sake of comparison.)

JUDY

Judy is a businesswoman in south Florida who had been married to Henry for twenty-four years. She said their marriage was like a Cinderella story. He was the first man she ever met and the first she ever dated. Against parental advice, they were engaged after their third date and married within six months.

Judy said that she never looked back; she was aware that she and Henry had something very special. "Other couples would be fighting and quarreling and we thought, you know, we just don't do that." She said that they would sit and talk about the fact that in all the years they were married they never fought. They were strong as a couple and also as individuals. They never competed with each other. They were happy and supported each other in their careers. They had similar interests, but when they had differences, compromise was easy. Judy said that they talked openly and freely to each other and felt safe sharing their ideas and emotions. They were "mentally tuned in to one another."

"I'm not talking about all the wonderful communication we had to deemphasize the physical side of the relationship. The two went together. I guess, in a word, good isn't good enough. It was perfect. I'm not just saying this because he's dead. We said that to each other when we were together." They had talked about death. They said that whoever went first would come back to be a guardian angel for the survivor.

Henry had always been in exceptional health. As Judy said, "Physical fitness was his thing." He was neat and trim and tidy, and he looked about fifteen years younger than his age. He came home one day from a business trip and said, "You know, my abdomen's sore. I guess it was too many sit-ups, what should I do?" She smiled and said, "Don't do so many sit-ups."

He returned from another business trip about three weeks later in what Judy described as "plain ordinary pain." He couldn't sleep that night, and he said, "You know, I think I need to see a doctor." That's when she knew something was wrong with him. Henry never went to the doctor.

It was late in the week when they went to the doctor's office. A variety of tests were ordered. The preliminary diagnostics, however, revealed nothing, so the physician decided to do more extensive testing on the coming Monday. Henry had a miserable, painful weekend. When he went in for his test on Monday, the severity of his condition was evident and the doctor decided to admit him to the hospital.

Judy related, "They ran every test known to man between Monday and that Friday. The doctors still couldn't prove anything. Because he was in so much pain, they concluded he had a ruptured appendix. They decided to go in and do an exploratory laparotomy. They opened him up and they looked inside."

His insides were covered with little tumors. The largest one was the size of a grain of rice, which is why they had never bothered him and could get so far without causing any symptoms. The doctors identified his condition as adenocarcinoma of the bowel, which is very difficult to treat. They did surgery on Friday.

After surgery, Henry demanded to know what they had found, and Judy told him. That was in October. He asked her, "What kind of time are we talking about?" She said, "We're not talking Christmas." Judy said that she was able to answer him so plainly because she was numb with grief and knew he wanted the truth. Then the doctors ordered one week of chemotherapy to see if it would have any impact at all. It didn't. Henry died three weeks after his surgery.

Within the first year of his death Judy had three vivid dreams of Henry. One was a visitation dream she had while staying at her mother's house.

"I can't remember where we were exactly. It was outside, in the woods or fields. We were talking, and we talked about life and other things. I remember that I was a little apprehensive about going on with my life without him. I told him this. He put his arms around me, and I could actually feel it in the dream. I've never felt anything in a dream before.

"This was so unlike other dreams. Regular dreams seem to move a little faster in terms of pace. It's sort of like taking a movie and winding it a little faster, speeding it up a little bit. But this was just a slow, everyday, normal pace of living kind of thing. A lot of times you'll have a dream that will cover a wide span of time in an incredibly short time frame.

"In this dream we had a lengthy discussion, but it wasn't rushed. Most people don't usually dream about two ordinary people just sitting and talking. Most dreams are action. I see other people, and most of them are kind of weird and bizarre like nightmares. But this was not. It was just plain, like you and I sitting and talking.

"When my husband and I were finished talking we stood up, and he just put his arms around me. It was that being touched and held feeling that woke me up. It was truly a phenomenal thing. It was so real. This dream said to me that though the person is not physically here, he's not really gone."

This dream helped Judy deal with her grief because it put her in touch with the spiritual nature of what had happened and showed her that there is something beyond death. She was painfully aware of Henry's physical absence, yet she knew his spirit was still with her. She said that she felt safer and more peaceful knowing this.

JUDY'S NONVISITATION DREAM

Judy had another memorable dream of Henry that was rich with symbolism. This was a nonvisitation dream and did not leave her with the sense that his spirit was present during the dream.

Several months after his death, she dreamed that she was living in a little house in the woods that overlooked the ocean. She had died in this dream, and her mother, who was living, came to her and said, "You know you have to leave this world and go to the other side. I'll walk with you down through the forest to the river that divides this world and the next." The river was small and was not flowing fast. There were small logs floating in the river. Judy jumped from one log to the next until she was on the other side.

Once across she saw all those who had gone before

her, her aunts and uncles, grandparents, and friends. Henry was there. Everyone greeted her. She knew that she was not yet in heaven, but in the place one goes before entering heaven.

Before they all moved into heaven they were to have lunch. She said it was like "something out of Fairyland." The table was sumptuous with magnificent ice carvings. When everyone was finished eating, they went into a huge room that had small beds all lined up. She and the others were to lie down and nap and once asleep would enter into heaven.

Judy remembers lying on the bed next to Henry: "He raised up on his elbow and said, 'By the way, Judy, what did you ever do about those things you needed to finish?' " Then he rattled off about five projects that I was supposed to have completed. I said, "Henry, I died. I couldn't finish those things." Then he told me I couldn't stay. He said, "You have to go back and finish those things."

Judy talked about the symbolism of the River Styx and the fact that she still did have things to do while living, though she missed him terribly. She said although this was a vivid dream, it was an ordinary dream. She did not feel that Henry had visited. Judy went on to say, "The ordinary dreams seem to actually have a lot more symbolism, while the visitation dream seemed a lot more straightforward."

Judy only had one more vivid but ordinary dream about Henry. She did have that one visitation dream, but on occasion, while awake she has felt his loving presence guiding her.

Many people have vivid dreams of someone who has died. In most cases they are ordinary dreams and deal with the loss or anxieties surrounding the loss. Shortly after her mother's death, Doreen had an ordinary dream about her. She was on a middle floor of a high-rise office building leaning out the window. She saw her mother falling in slow motion past her, toward the ground, and realized there was nothing she could do to help her because her mother was out of reach.

Doreen awoke shaken but was able to interpret the dream to mean that there was really nothing she could have done to alter the course of her mother's illness and subsequent death. Nonvisitation dreams, like visitation dreams can leave a lasting impression and prove to help the survivor deal with grief. In Judy's case her nonvisitation dreams reminded her of Henry, brought back feelings associated with him, and helped her find reasons for going on without him. It was the visitation dream that affirmed his spirit was still alive and that her spirit would also live, and it was the visitation dream that gave her a sense of peace, during the dream and after.

Both types of dreams can help resolve grief, but no matter how vivid a nonvisitation dream or how simple a visitation dream, when asked, the dreamer will be able to distinguish between the two.

As well as affirming that the spirit of the dead person is still alive, the visitation dreams can provide information to resolve unanswered questions.

LINDA

Linda is a delightfully eccentric writer in her early forties. She is divorced and has two teenage children. She loves her family, and they play an important role in her life. When her grandmother died, she felt the loss intensely because her grandmother had been like a second mother to her.

Her grandmother grew up in Florida in a family that did not believe in educating women. She left her home at twelve and lied about her age to get a job and send herself to night school. She lived in an attic apartment, and for three years her diet was primarily peanut butter and bread.

When she was seventeen, she married a man who was fifty-six years old and quite well-to-do. But after Linda's mother was born, he lost all his money. Linda's grandmother, however, had saved $3,000 in cash, and when the banks crashed during the depression, the grandparents used this money to start a restaurant. Her grandmother ran the business, and the family restaurant did very well. She remained frugal, however.

After Linda's mother had grown up and moved out, her grandparents moved from their stately home to a comfortable two-bedroom house. Linda's grandmother played an active role in raising Linda and her brother and sister. Linda would sometimes accompany her grandmother to work. She would often go to her grandmother's house to spend the day when she was a child. Linda was especially fond of the house where she remembers learning to cook with her grandmother. It held many wonderful memories for her.

It was a small brick house with a screened porch. Linda remembers sitting on the porch with her grandmother. Her grandmother had a green thumb and filled the porch with beautiful plants. Small chameleons used to come in and sun themselves on the leaves of the plants. Linda used to like to watch them change color as they moved from the green plants to the screen.

Linda and her siblings would play in the garden behind the house. They planted flowers all around the backyard. She said that they even replanted weeds that had pretty flowers. Linda distinctly remembered the holly bush that bloomed at Christmastime. She would take pieces of holly and place it in vases around the house for holiday color.

When her grandmother asked Linda what she wanted to inherit after her death, Linda always replied "I want this house." But when Linda's grandmother died, she had specified in her will that the house would be sold. Linda was understandably disappointed and began to drive by the house, remembering all the time she had spent there.

Several years later, Linda, now divorced with two children, received money from the trust fund her grandmother had left to her to buy a new house.

One night shortly thereafter Linda had a visitation dream of her grandmother. She and her grandmother were standing in front of the small brick house. Her grandmother looked beautiful and peaceful and smiled lovingly at her. Linda was not afraid and related that she also felt a peacefulness. Her grandmother proceeded to take Linda through the house, room by room. In each room she pointed out why this would not have been a good house for her granddaughter. She explained that central heat and air-conditioning would have to be installed and that this work would be a significant expense. The backyard would be too small for Linda's son to play ball. She also pointed out how close the bedrooms were to the living room. She explained that this was fine for an elderly woman who had people visit once in a while, but it would never offer enough space or privacy for a young mother and children.

Linda remembers following her grandmother through the house as vividly as if it were happening today. As they went through each room, Linda finally understood and accepted that this was not the house for her. After this dream, Linda was peaceful with her grandmother's decision about the sale of the house. She also gained a new appreciation for her newly bought home and realized that it was her grandmother's real gift to her.

Linda's dream had given her insights into her grandmother's thinking. Having this information, she was able to resolve her sadness over not owning the old house. The dream helped her focus on what she had now. She stopped longing for the past and began enjoying her new house. She also became more aware of her grandmother's loving spirit. After that dream Linda began to trust that events happening around her were probably happening for a reason. In a sense the dream gave her an optimistic way to view life and an ability to believe in life after death.

JEAN

Jean, book editor and mother of three, believes that ADC has helped put her into a serene mind set about death. She is no longer afraid of it for reasons that are obvious from her description. In fact, Jean sees death as a bridge between one world and another. Her attitude and her husband's are so open that she knows her young children will grow up without ever doubting the probability of an afterlife and the possibility of maintaining relationships with loved ones after they have departed.

"My mother had one sister, we called her Weddy-Pooh. She lived with my grandmother close by, and when I was home raising my children, I would visit them every day to take them to the store and check in on them. My aunt was diagnosed as a manic-depressive and was in bed most of the time for the last ten years of her life. One day my grandmother called me and said that Weddy-Pooh had died in her sleep; she asked me to come over and make sure, which I did. She had indeed died.

"About two years later I had a dream of Weddy-Pooh. She was all 'spruced up' as she would say, running through the clouds, dressed in a new dress with a leather handbag and new shoes. The quality of clothing was always important to her, particularly when she wasn't depressed. She waved and kept going, and I

called out, 'Weddy-Pooh can't you stop for a while?'
She told me she couldn't stop because she had to go
somewhere in a hurry. She was going to pick up one of
the 'sisters.' I interpreted this to mean my grandmother
or her only living sister, Mary. There had been seven
sisters, and at one time during their adulthood, they
had all lived together in a small town in Oklahoma.

"Right then I got up, and said to my husband, 'I've
got to call my mother because either Grandma died or
Aunt Mary (her sister) died, and Aunt Weddy-Pooh
was going to get one of them in my dream.' I wanted to
verify it immediately.

"Upon phoning my mother, I learned that it was
Aunt Mary who had died in the night."

Jean also related a dream her father had of his
deceased sister.

"My brother and his baby were killed by a drunk dri-
ver and my father could not recover from his over-
whelming grief. He felt like he had failed somehow to
protect them like a father wants to protect his children.
He was in emotional agony. Then his twin sister died a
little more than one year later. Exactly six months to
the day on the anniversary of her death, my family had
planned a memorial service for her. In the middle of the
night, my dad had a dream where she appeared to him
and said, 'Joe, you didn't set your alarm clock for my
memorial service and you better do that; otherwise, you
won't make it to the service.'

"Then he asked her how it was going. At this point,
my father told me, his twin sister became ecstatic; just

thinking about how much fun she was having made her glow. 'I can go anywhere I want,' she said, 'at any time I want. I'm having so much fun. I can go to California and Hawaii whenever I want. I can't wait until you join me. You're going to love it, Joe.'

"Sure enough he got up and his alarm wasn't set. He set it, went to her memorial service, and one week later, he died. I'm so grateful he shared this experience with me before he died."

KATIE

Katie, a young widow, described a dream of her thirty-four-year-old husband, Matt, who died in a mountain-climbing accident. Matt had always loved the outdoors. He and Katie were accomplished climbers and scheduled vacations where they could climb, finally deciding to move from New York State to Colorado for more opportunities to enjoy their sport.

One day Matt went climbing with some of his friends and made a technical error that sent him falling to his death. Though his friends told Katie his death was merciful, she didn't quite believe them.

Then Katie was visited by Matt in a dream. "The most vivid [visitation] dream I had was a couple of nights after he had died. It took place in the mountains, in a spot he loved. In the dream he knew he was dead, and I knew he was dead. It was an opportunity for him to talk to me. He very much wanted to make sure I was okay and to reassure me that he was going to be okay.

He let me know that his death had been quick and he did not suffer.

"Though he didn't say it, I knew I wouldn't see him again. This was sad but I also knew he was with me spiritually and that I would be reunited with him after I died. We didn't talk much, but I felt his love. We looked at each other, and he took my hand. I could almost feel it. Then somehow we both knew it was time for him to go. He gave me a tender smile that melted my heart. It was sad and wonderful at the same time. Then I just dissolved into the darkness of sleep. That dream gave us time together. It was a beautiful way to say good-bye."

This visitation dream was simple, but powerful, in that it served as a vehicle for Katie to process her grief. In general, after having a visitation dream, the survivor usually feels more peaceful. Visitation dreams, like other forms of ADC, help survivors through their grief. They also affirm that the loved one's spirit remains alive. The dreams give helpful advice and support and facilitate change.

Four

Feelings Associated with ADC

ADC evokes different emotions. Many people say they feel calm while it is occurring and accept what is happening, as they would any other experience. They will say: "It was no big deal," or "It's just something that happens." The matter-of-fact attitude many people have surprised me while I was doing my research. After they think about the experience, most people feel joy, happiness, and comfort. However, some have negative or incongruent feelings. Occasionally someone will experience feelings of intense grief, experiencing the same emotions they had when the person died.

Matter-of-Fact Acceptance

ADC makes people feel close to the deceased, but remarkably, a number of people I spoke to felt quite dispassionate during the experience. After the death of his beloved wife, Joy Davidson, the author C. S. Lewis had a dream about her. In his journal he describes the feelings during the dream, writing that the quality of the experience made it notable: "It was quite incredibly unemotional. Just the impression of her mind momentarily facing my own." He continued, "One didn't need emotion. The intimacy was complete—sharply bracing and restorative, too—without it. Can that intimacy be love itself—always in this life attended with emotion, not because it is itself an emotion, or needs an attendant emotion, but because our animal souls, our nervous systems, our imaginations, have to respond to it in that way?"

Many people I spoke to said that during the experience they felt relatively little emotion; the emotion came later as they reflected on what had happened. Thus people often describe their experiences matter-of-factly. As one woman said, "When I say it's not on an emotional level, I don't mean that in a negative sense. I'm meaning that it's almost a mental thing. It's logical; it's unemotional. There's not a positive feeling, like happy and glad and bouncing around, nor is there a negative or sad feeling. It's peaceful, it's rational, it's wonderful."

MARCIA

Marcia had expected Victor's death. He had multiple medical problems including end-stage Alzheimer's disease. She told people that her husband's death was a "blessing." Those she knew assumed Marcia was relieved because he had been so difficult and she would get over the death quickly. In reality, she was deeply saddened by it and questioned herself about what else she could have done for him. Even though he was in a nursing home, Victor's care had dictated her routine. She found purpose in these activities.

One evening a few weeks after the funeral, Marcia was sitting quietly after talking on the phone to her daughter. She was considering her daughter's proposal to move to Baltimore and live in the one-bedroom apartment she and her husband owned. At the same time she began reminiscing about all she and Victor had done in this house. She missed him and their life together. She closed her eyes for a minute, and when she opened them, she saw Victor sitting on the sofa. She said:

"He was on the old plaid couch, facing me. He smiled and nodded, as if to say, 'I know. We had a good life here.' It's funny I didn't get excited. I felt calm. He didn't have to talk; we were in touch without that. He stayed a couple minutes then disappeared.

"When I think about it, I guess I should be more excited, even now. Here was my dead husband, and I'm acting like this is par for the course. But, you know, it was so natural. I didn't feel strange, and the whole thing didn't seem like a big deal. I never questioned it. I never questioned myself. I got a great deal of comfort from that visit, even though I never expected it."

For most people, "peaceful" best describes how they feel during the experience because this extraordinary event seems perfectly rational while it's happening, and ultimately they feel good about it.

Feeling Positive

Despite their effortless acceptance of ADC while it's happening, when people later reflect on the experience, they tend to have difficulty describing their emotions. ADC generally does not evoke fear because the experience is so far removed from their everyday life. Many say it evokes a special feeling. Gail, who was mentioned earlier as experiencing her mother through the sense of smell, described her reaction this way: "It was like a lifting up of your soul, you know, inspirational. But not really like religious experiences I've had, like when the preacher is saying something, and I might get chills all over my body. They're both great feelings, but different. It [ADC] was such a good feeling; I just couldn't think anything negative could come from that kind of feeling."

One consistent feeling people pinpoint is being comforted, about their grief over the death itself, as well as other feelings of sadness and worry.

ELLEN

Ellen recounted to me her mother's experience with her grandmother. The family owned an antebellum home in Jefferson County, Virginia, which had been in the family for years. Ellen remembered the house with great fondness and warmth. In the 1960s the family decided to sell the home because it was becoming too much for Ellen's aging aunt and uncle who lived there to maintain. Ellen and her mother spent one last weekend at the family home. That night, as Ellen's mother was lying in bed, she felt someone hug her, and then she felt a taffeta dress brush her skin. She knew this was Ellen's grandmother, who had died years before. Ellen's mother felt comforted and knew that her mother was consoling her about selling the home.

ANDIE

Andie had a similar experience when she finally donated her deceased mother's clothing to a charity. She had been torn for several years about parting with her mother's wardrobe. Her garments hung in the closet just as they had when her mother was alive. "It became almost like a shrine," Andie said. "And we were running out of room for our own clothing. I knew it was time to put the living first, but I felt so guilty about it."

As Andie explains, she was carefully removing the dresses from hangers when her mother appeared to her. "She was dressed entirely in a glistening light. It was the most beautiful dress I'd ever seen. I only saw her for a second, but I knew right away it was her way of giving me permission to throw all the old junk out. After all, what did she need with this old stuff when she was dressed in something as magnificent as that. It was funny, really."

Andie's example not only typifies the comfort many feel, but also the comic nature of some connections. Often, a loved one's sense of humor proves to be enduring.

Almost everyone is happy that they have had the experience and believe it helps their grief. One woman said: "For me, it lessened the grief process. Because part of grief is that you have someone in your life and you're with them all the time, and all of a sudden they're gone. You can't depend on that form of communication, that relationship, for something you've been used to in your life. So that when you can still talk to them, then you don't grieve so much because they're still there for you in a way. It's not like they've been taken or like you've lost something so much."

Beyond the comforting feeling ADC provides, it also inspires wonder and awe.

KYLE

Kyle was in college when his mother died. He said, "I thought I was handling her death pretty well, but I was in denial. I wasn't processing her death well. I didn't cry or deal with my emotions. I just got morose."

The semester after his mother died he took an existential literature class. He said, "We read people like Camus and Sartre. I think their beliefs on the meaningless of human life gave me the fodder I needed to really go into a depression over Mom's death. Nothing was making sense anyway, and here these guys give me permission to see the absurdity of life itself."

One night about six weeks into the semester, Kyle had a visitation dream of his mother. It took place in the garden behind the family home. He said:

"She was standing in the garden, surrounded by sunlight and flowers. I could feel her presence there; I knew it was really her. That was her garden; she loved it. When I was a kid and couldn't find her in the house, I knew I could find her there, pruning something or planting something. I wasn't surprised this is where I saw her.

"While I was dreaming everything seemed perfectly normal. She looked happy. All she said was, 'It's magnificent.' I knew she wasn't talking about the garden even though it was magnificent, full of wildflowers and butterflies. That simple statement struck a chord. All of a sudden in the dream, I felt like I was covered in sunlight, too.

"When I woke up I heard her voice in my head, 'It's magnificent.' I knew that there is something beyond our 'meaningless' lives. And I knew I did not invent this dream to give my life meaning. I couldn't have invented it. I was in no shape to do it. This other realm is there. It's independent of human thought. Seeing her inspired me beyond words. It was awesome. She's right. It is magnificent."

Feeling Negative

When someone had conflicted relationship with the deceased, sometimes they reexperience that conflict with the deceased. Their feelings on these occasions are like those anyone would have with a living person. This typically occurs when the survivor is addressing unresolved issues with the deceased, but even those who have negative feelings when communicating with the deceased also have positive feelings at other times.

SAM

Sam, a physician's assistant, said this about his mother who had died with chronic obstructive pulmonary disease: "I think that because we had so much unfinished business, the initial experiences with her were not all that pleasant. I had a lot of anger and guilt, and it overflowed into those encounters. When I felt her presence, it was like, 'Oh no, let's not go through this again.' Strangely enough, our relationship has changed, and now it's a different kind of presence, more comforting."

Some people who had ongoing experiences felt good about them sometimes and felt troubled at others.

THERESA

Theresa and John had known each other since they were children. They married shortly before World War II. Theresa said she had no frame of reference when John died of cancer at thirty-six. She thought he was indestructible. While in the war, John had been taken prisoner in the Philippines. He endured terrific hardships but survived and returned to her. She said, "I can't believe he lived through that and died of cancer so young."

Before John and Theresa got married, they promised each other that if one of them become terminally ill, the healthy spouse would hold the sick one at the moment of death. Theresa was not able to be in the hospital when John died and therefore could not keep her promise:

"The first time I saw him after he died, he said, 'How could you?' He was talking about me breaking the promise and not being with him when he died. I felt awful. I tried to explain. That was very difficult for me.

"But other times I see him or hear him and I feel good. Sometimes we have simple chats about nothing important; sometimes he'll just touch me."

Theresa continues to deal with interpersonal issues in an ongoing relationship with John. They discuss such things as their children, what they could have done differently while married, and how they are going to meet after Theresa dies. Most of these experiences are warm and loving; some remind her that she was not with him at the time of his death. Her relationship with him is still very much alive: "You know, I still feel him kiss me every night before I go to sleep."

Having a good experience with the deceased, while still grieving for them, seems incongruous to some people. They can't reconcile their feelings of happiness, closeness, and joy from the experience with the grief they still have. They describe it as "weird" and "incongruous." Some people express guilt for having positive feelings. They feel constrained by their grief to limit themselves to certain feelings.

EDWARD

Edward, a lawyer in his early seventies, said: "When I heard my wife calling my name I was so excited and happy. I wanted to tell the kids, 'Guess what just happened to me?' But this was a week after we buried their mother, and somehow my excitement seemed inappropriate when I thought how they might react. And after I had that feeling I felt guilty for being elated while my wife had just been buried. I felt like I should be more reserved, more reverent."

An elderly widow also had negative experiences when her husband returned to her. "Sensing him here was just too difficult. It reminded me that I couldn't really have him, so I didn't want it to happen at all."

JENIFER

Jenifer, a patient from my private practice, had a different experience, although also negative. She told me she felt guilty for holding her husband back. She felt her terrible grief made it hard for him to leave and move on spiritually. "I'd cry myself to sleep and feel his heavy presence all around me. I knew he was supposed to move on, but he was staying around to comfort me. It made me feel worse, and I prayed that he'd feel free to leave me so he could grow. When I felt his spirit finally leave, I actually felt better. I know we'll be together again."

Jenifer's way of coping illustrates a healthy response. Even though her husband was deceased, she felt empowered by her ability to do something for him. Although he was gone she believed she could still facilitate his spiritual growth. In this way she was able to let go of him selflessly, knowing that their spiritual connection was eternal. Also, her own growth was facilitated by the experience.

Reexperiencing Feelings of Loss

Though most people don't feel that ADC is a painful reminder of the deceased's absence, some feel as if they lose the deceased all over again when the experience ends. These feelings can be as intense as those they first had when the person died, without the support of the mourning rituals. All of the participants in my research were glad they had had the experience, but those who reexperienced grief did not always want another experience.

VERA

Vera is a piano teacher in her thirties who experienced her father. She said, "I couldn't have felt any worse, and I think that's why he came, but it was so painful to let him go again." Losing him after her experience was more difficult than his death because she felt alone and without support during the experience: "Not that I wouldn't love for my daddy to come in and sit down and be here . . . when he came to me that was the relief, but when he then started moving away, and I couldn't stop him. . . . He said everything would be all right, and he said, 'You're going to be all right.' And, then I said, I didn't think so, because I was really worried about how I was going to take care of my mother. I told him, 'I don't think so, so please don't go away.' And he said 'now you're going to be all right.' And then he started fading. I said, 'Don't go,' and I reached out my hand, and he reached his out; I asked, 'Will I see you again?' He just had this sweet peaceful look on his face and drifted away. Then that feeling was terrible, because there's nothing you can do. So I don't want to go through that again.

"When someone dies, you have the funeral, everybody's around, it's kind of a busy time. There's a lot going on, and people know you're grieving, so people are sharing that with you. But when you have a presence, they [the deceased] come and they go, and then you're alone; you don't go around talking about it."

There was no one with whom to share her feelings. She felt her loss deeply and did not believe she could approach others to talk about what she was going through. As it becomes more widely known that ADC is a regular phenomenon associated with grief, people will begin to feel comfortable seeking help from family, friends, or professionals when reexperiencing their initial grief.

Yet, most people are thankful for the reconnection and occasionally a little fearful that they will not be able to remember the feelings associated with the experience.

Five

The Deceased's Familiar Cues

Because after-death contact is outside the boundaries of "normal" experience, people may subtly question themselves about it. Although the bereaved immediately recognize the deceased through a sixth sense, they can second-guess this intuitive way of knowing. For this reason, many believe the deceased identify themselves with specific cues. For example, they may return wearing a favorite dress, smoking a specific brand of tobacco, or in the company of a beloved dog. They may also address the bereaved with a favorite nickname.

Psychiatrist C. G. Jung, who is perhaps most famous for his extensive work with dreams, also had a visitation dream of his wife. In his book *Memories, Dreams, and Reflections,* he writes of recognizing a certain dress his wife was wearing during the ADC:

"After the death of my wife I saw her in a dream which was like a vision. She stood at some distance from me, looking at me squarely. She was in her prime, perhaps about thirty, and wearing the dress which had been made for her many years before. It was perhaps the most beautiful thing she had ever worn. Her expression was neither joyful nor sad, but, rather objectively wise and understanding, without the slightest emotional reaction, as though she was beyond the mist of affects."

ANDREW

Andrew, a mechanic, said that seeing his deceased grandfather smoking a pipe and wearing the flannel shirt he used to frequently wear made the experience authentic for him. He said, "I think seeing him in those clothes and with that pipe let me know it was real. I might have questioned my sanity if he were wearing a suit. I would wonder who I was seeing. I recognized that old shirt and the pipe he used to carry around even when he wasn't smoking it."

Another person said, "I can see her sitting there in my car, like a shadow. She always wears things that she had from years before she died. She's not in today's clothes."

Finding people in the clothes of their time is a common theme, allowing the bereaved to identify the loved one. The visual cue forms a bridge to the past. One woman said, "I know Gramma probably doesn't even wear clothes now, but I bet she thought it would make me feel better and help me recognize her. I don't think I ever saw her without that apron, so when I saw it, I knew her in a second."

One woman who later had her own experiences with her mother was given a message from her minister who had an ADC with her shortly after the funeral.

JILL

Jill is an inspirational speaker. When she was twenty-eight years old her mother, Marie, who was an alcoholic, committed suicide. Her death was a shock to the whole family and difficult for Jill to endure.

When Jill was young her mother used to threaten suicide frequently. Jill remembers her father going to great lengths to thwart Marie's attempts. Once he went so far as nailing the garage door shut, so she could not get in to use the automobile's carbon monoxide to kill herself, and mixing water in the vodka bottles so she would not drink herself to death.

As years went by, she stopped threatening to take her life, but she kept drinking. As Marie kept drinking, she became more depressed. Then one morning without any apparent warning, Marie committed suicide by shooting herself in the head.

At the funeral Jill remembers standing by the casket stroking her mother's hair and saying "Mom I can't think of anything good to remember you by." At first she could not believe that her mother was gone. As time went by she became angry and would think, "I hope you're happy now, now that we can't fight anymore because you're gone." At times she would question, "Why did this happen?" She felt a mixture of emotions, including deep sorrow.

As Jill was working through her grief, the minister from her church approached her and said, "Your mother came to me. She said that she wants you to remember her as she was sixteen years ago. That is the way she is now." Her mother told him that when you die you can go to the time when you were the happiest. Jill remembered that sixteen years before her mother's death was a happy time for the whole family. This statement the minister heard was the cue Jill needed to know her mother did indeed speak to him. It also told her that her mother was in a sense answering a prayer by giving her something good to remember her by.

The familiar cues are a very comforting part of the experience, and the following case illustrates the deceased using familiar vocal cues to connect and comfort.

SARA

I interviewed Sara several years ago in the hospital. She was a nurse and was working in psychiatry on the same unit where I was supervising nursing students. She knew about my research and volunteered to talk with me. She told me about her experience with her mother while we had a quick lunch break together in the nursing station.

Sara had lost both her mother and father in a traumatic accident. Her father was a trucker. He and her mother were on an eighteen-wheel rig in the Carolina mountains when the truck lost its brakes. Her father was unable to maintain control of the vehicle, and they crashed. Sara, who had just graduated from high school, was aware of the details of their deaths, but was relieved to know that they both died instantly.

A few months later, Sara was at her parents' home, getting ready to go out. It was around five P.M., and she was brushing her teeth when she distinctly heard her mother call her name. The voice was so distinct that she dropped her toothbrush and started to search the house for her mother. She knew immediately that it was her mother. Not only was it clearly her mother's voice but also her mother had called Sara by the nickname she had always used. Hearing the familiar nickname and her mother's voice let Sara know that her mother was all right.

In the following example, Martha's grandmother relied on visual cues to calm and connect with her.

MARTHA

Martha was six years old when her grandmother died. She still remembers that time vividly and describes it warmly: "My grandmother died at home. I remember one day she was there, and suddenly she was gone. Because this was in the 1940s and I was just a child, I was insulated from what was going on. So the next thing I remember is seeing Grandmother at the funeral home in the coffin. Because she died at home, I had gotten used to her changing countenance over the course of her illness. But seeing her at the funeral home was the most ghastly thing I had ever witnessed in my life. She did not look at all like my grandmother. She had this beautifully preserved looking skin, even smoothed out a little bit. I'm not sure how they did that, but I didn't see the old familiar wrinkles. It was a disturbing experience. And when my aunt said, 'Don't you want to touch her?' I said, 'No, that isn't my grandmother.'

"But, when I saw my grandmother during the experience it was totally different. I had just run to my bedroom to put on my tennis shoes. I was sitting on the bed lacing them up when I happened to glance up into the doorway and there she was, wearing the same blue dress that she had on at the funeral parlor. She looked natural, not so made-up. This was my grandmother. This beautiful spirit was much more my grandmother than that made-up body I had seen at the funeral parlor."

At another time Martha's mother also saw Martha's grandmother. When she saw Martha's grandmother she was dressed in white, different clothes than Martha had seen her in. Martha said, "Grandmother loved my mother very much. I'm sure Grandmother was looking in on her and reassuring her that she was coming from a heavenly place. That's why when mother saw her she was in white. When I saw her it was just the way I had remembered seeing her the last time. I think I saw her the way I did because I needed to be able to recognize her."

Recognizing the deceased is also made easier if the experience is compatible with the way in which the survivor knew the deceased. One woman said about her deceased mother: "I felt her presence when I was sitting at home, close to where she used to read. That made me feel like this made sense. It was really her."

NATALIE

Natalie was in her first year at college when her little brother, Jerry, died. She said the events surrounding his death were unclear, and no one was sure if his death had been accidental or a suicide. He was a senior in high school and had been out drinking with friends on a Saturday night. His friends took him to the emergency room after he collapsed. On autopsy it was discovered he not only had high alcohol blood levels but also had ingested sedatives. His friends said they knew he was drunk, but knew nothing about the drugs. Natalie said:

"Mom died of cancer a couple of years before. Jerry seemed to do pretty well at first. In retrospect, he probably did too well. You know, I don't think he was dealing with it. He started running with a pretty rough crowd, for our small town. Dad and I worried about him. We suspected he was depressed, but had no clue how bad. The alcohol only made things worse.

"Up until Mom's death, Jerry loved being in the woods, anything to do with nature. He had a couple close friends he would hunt and fish with. The bad things he used to do were sneaking out of the house before dawn to go fishing, or coming in way too late after a hunting trip; now it was drinking. He had really changed.

"After he died, I started coming home more on weekends. Dad and I each got help, to deal with the grief and the guilt. When I was home we would sit and talk, try to comfort each other. We reminisced about the good times, and tried to make new ones."

Natalie said she was at home about a month after Jerry died. She was just waking up. The door to her room was open, and she could look out into the hallway and see the doors to the bathroom and linen closet. The rising sun cast shadows in the hall. Natalie said:

"I happened to glance out into the hall. I didn't pay much attention, but noticed the light looked a little strange. Then I looked again. I saw this transparent figure; it was Jerry. It was like he was made of light, but it was clearly him. He was dressed in clothes like he wore when he went into the woods. They looked like light too, but you could see a pattern. He had a smile and was rummaging through the linen closet.

"This was so amazing! I had seen him do that so many times before. He would look for pillowcases to put his catch in. He used to get in trouble for using the good pillowcases for God knows what, snakes, turtles. You name it."

Natalie went on to explain that seeing her brother engaged in this activity was so meaningful, not only because she saw him doing something he liked, but because it made sense he would be searching the linen closet. It was compatible with the way she knew him.

The total experience, however, does not have to be congruent with the way in which the person had interacted with the deceased while alive. In fact, many of the ways in which the people have experienced the deceased would seem bizarre to someone who never has. It is easier for survivors to accept ADC when elements of the experience are contextually congruent. One woman said that she would question an experience if her deceased husband came to her in an unfamiliar way.

Deborah, whose experience was described earlier, felt her bed moving in the rhythm of her husband's heartbeat. She felt that this was an acceptable way to experience him because they had a physical, loving relationship: "I think that it was very meaningful that he died of congestive heart failure and that the bed was moving in the rhythm of his heart beating. I think it was so meaningful; if I had seen him standing there, maybe I would have questioned my sanity and the experience at that point."

Although Deborah says she would question her sanity, the reality is that everyone I spoke to ultimately accepted the experience as real. What's more, they felt comforted and inspired by it. Experiencing the loved one in a familiar way, often vibrant and strong, is a healthy and loving way to remember that person. Without this positive experience, the bereaved might cling to psychologically troubling memories that could impede the grief process.

When working with grieving individuals, it is not unusual to help them balance their memories of the deceased. When faced with lingering recollections that are particularly sad, gruesome, or angry, I will help the survivor discover healthier, happier, or more loving ways to relate to the deceased. This is something ADCs do naturally.

LISA

Lisa and Scott had been married for two years. They had met while Scott was speaking at a group for newly diagnosed diabetics that Lisa attended. Her diabetes was easily controlled by oral medication, but Scott's was more problematic. He had to take insulin injections and sometimes needed doctor visits for readjustment of the dose. Nevertheless, he was a model patient and was proud of his healthy lifestyle.

They both enjoyed cooking and liked coming up with inventive recipes that were appropriate for their diets. One evening Scott was preparing the grill. Lisa said:

"I don't really know what happened, but I heard this scream. When I looked out on the patio I saw Scott ripping off his Hawaiian shirt; it was in flames. I grabbed the extinguisher from the kitchen and a throw from the couch as I ran by it. My mind was racing. When I got to him, he was out of his shirt, but was burned pretty bad. I called 911.

"The next few days were a blur. He had all kinds of complications and died four days after he was admitted. I had nightmares for a week. I relived the fire. In one of the dreams I was the one who caused it. I woke up in a cold sweat with my heart pounding. I was afraid to sleep because of the nightmares, but didn't want to be awake either and feel the pain of the loss. I didn't want to take sleeping pills because I was too afraid my dreams would only be worse and it would be harder to wake up from them."

Then Lisa explained that after about a week of nightmares she had a visitation dream. She said:

"I saw him standing in the living room, looking out at the patio. I walked over to him and he took my hand. Everything was calm. We both knew he was dead, but that didn't seem to matter. He said, 'You see, I'm fine. All you need to do is love me. I'm fine.' In the dream I said to him 'I miss you.' And he said 'I'm in your heart.' Then he squeezed my hand and disappeared.

"I woke up from this dream too, but my heart wasn't pounding, I wasn't sweating. I knew he had been with me. I thought he was telling me to think of him in a loving way so I would stop having nightmares. I felt calm, relieved. I had a new image, a new way to see him."

Experiencing the deceased in such a positive light helps survivors with their grief because it facilitates letting go of sadness, guilt, or other negative emotions perpetuated by negative memories. ADCs present an optimistic picture of existence beyond the confines of the physical.

Six

Comprehending the Private Reality

Two major inner tools we use to comprehend the world around us are rational thought and intuition. Rational thought allows us to order our lives through categorization and logical reasoning. We rely on it as a means of objectively analyzing our experiences, believing in the reality of our experience, and taking action.

Intuition on the other hand provides a basis for belief and action that is outside the realm of logical thought. It is associative, not deductive. It is creative not scientific. Intuition allows us to know about something without any rational basis for that knowledge: that a distant loved one is happy, sad, or hurt; that an apparently safe situation is dangerous, or vice versa.

Our belief system is made up of the thoughts we subscribe to. These thoughts can be constructed of both rational thoughts and intuitive thoughts. They can either help us interpret events in a positive manner or present us with frightening realities of our own making. As we grow, we develop belief systems about ourselves and the world around us. This process is partially unconscious. Many of the beliefs are passed down to us. I often hear people say, "Oh, I'm sounding just like my mother." Our beliefs are also received from and influenced by teachers, peers, life experiences, and so on. We weave these ideas about reality together and develop an internal, intellectual structure through which we relate to the world we live in. Of course, if we reflect on our beliefs, we can revise them as we gain information and go through life.

Intuition

Intuition is one mode of belief not passed down to us. It plays an important role in balancing our belief systems by providing a sense that not everything is quantitatively knowable. For example, people raised in a prejudiced home may continue to think prejudiced thoughts even in the face of opposing ideas. Their intuition, however, may let them know, "This does not really feel right." People would be well served if they listened to this voice more often.

PAT

Pat, a physician friend who practices internal medicine, comes to mind. A patient came to her still grieving after her husband had died of lung cancer, complaining of a constant state of exhaustion. Of course, Pat recognized this complaint as a common symptom of depression. The woman thought she might also have lung cancer. Not understanding cancer well, the woman pointed to an extremely small mole on her hand as evidence that the cancer had spread. Although the woman's reasoning was faulty and the mole didn't display the characteristic signs of a melanoma, Pat's intuition told her to pursue it. Her intuition combined with her patient's proved to be right. The mole was cancerous, and it was removed immediately.

Despite all outward appearances that the woman was somatically preoccupied, Pat sensed something about the mole. No external cues gave her this information. In fact, all the external cues pointed in the opposite direction. The woman had just had a complete workup and everything had been within normal limits. However, it is not unusual for the bereaved to imagine they have symptoms similar to the deceased. In light of the woman's health status, state of bereavement, and the benign characteristics of the mole, it would have been within the range of acceptable medical procedures for Pat to make a note to reinspect the mole later. Yet an intuitive voice guided her. Pat told me that her intuition often guides her in her work and that it's amazingly accurate.

I continually see examples of the power of intuition throughout my private practice. Patients act on wild hunches only to find they're true. One such patient actually located a sister's lost manuscript when its whereabouts came to her in a dream. The manuscript had slipped behind a mat in her sister's trunk and remained lodged there for several weeks until my patient found it in a dream. We may not understand where intuitive information comes from, but even police departments across the country rely upon people with special intuitive skills to help them crack cases. These people are truly the undercover agents. Because of the controversial nature of their work, however, their contributions are rarely discussed openly. I have, however, counseled patients in my private practice who have worked side by side with gifted intuitives, and their information can be startlingly accurate.

When survivors make sense of ADCs using their intuition, I find that it gives them a tremendous amount of strength. Opening to divine possibilities infuses the grieving process with a sense of hope for their loved ones and for them.

ADC Has Spiritual Consequences

Most people I spoke to believe ADC is spiritual in nature. One woman who worked at a hospice said that she had been "blessed with strong faith." "It's not a rational thing: it's pretty irrational, but it sustains me. If I were asked, if the sum of all my experiences working at a hospice, and being with people who were dying had any influence on my faith, the answer would be yes. It affirmed that there's something that happens, and that it isn't bad. It was kind of like being able to get a glimpse of what is beyond what you normally don't get to see. There are so many synchronistic events that surround many of the death experiences that defy all logic." All of these synchronistic events, including her own experience, fit with her belief system. She did not try to examine these events or dissect them in a scientific way, but rather thought about them in terms of her faith.

Nadia, a midwife who has studied the writings of Carl Jung and experienced her father, said that it is important to just accept some of the "mysteries of life." She felt "privileged to engage in one of life's mysteries." In another case a young equestrienne with strong spiritual beliefs lost her close friend in a tragic automobile accident. When speaking of her experience with her friend, she said, "This is something that you just can't look into too hard. It just happens. It speaks for itself."

Those who believe in spiritual explanations find spiritual consequences from the experience. For most, the consequences fit easily with their spiritual beliefs. Others are forced to examine some of their values. Many say that the experience gives them a better sense of what is important in life. One woman said smilingly that the experience gave her "a much larger outline to work with." She no longer worried "about the trivial things," which she found comforting, and consequently felt more at peace with herself. Curtis, a small-business owner, said his experience "put things in perspective" for him. It helped him see what was important and that his life is only a small part of a greater reality: "It humbles you. It helps you relate to reality a little differently. It gives you this sense that things you used to think were so important maybe aren't as important as you thought."

When survivors believe that their ADC is real, it makes them want to lead more spiritual lives. They are reminded of the importance of what they are doing on earth. A nursing professor, who was already quite active in her church, felt a heightened need to know what she was "supposed to do while alive." "I think it strengthened my value system. I now would like to be more open while on this earth. I feel closer to the spiritual side of life. I want to be more Christlike than humanlike."

However, even those who experienced ADCs spiritually still felt conflicted at times. As Terri, a grade school teacher and a patient of mine, said, "I knew that this [ADC] was spiritual; I could feel it, so I felt blessed. But at the same time I had been raised with the notion that all the good souls were in heaven after they die. Honestly, it was this one instance that was so different than what I learned. It pointed out to me 'Girl, you better think about God differently.' " Terri examined what she had been taught as a child and found much of her belief system quite limiting. She refashioned her beliefs to be more positive, and this change led her to be a more loving person to herself and to others.

ADC makes the spiritual realm more accessible. The authentic nature of the experience provides acceptable evidence of existence after death. When people view life and death less dichotomously, death is not as frightening. People sense a continuity from one realm to the next. One woman said about heaven: "I guess some people have never thought of the possibility that maybe there and here are the same place." Survivors often say that after ADC, they feel closer to the deceased. Some even feel closer to God. One woman said, "The reconnection was like a spark. It was mysterious and wonderful and made me feel close to the deceased. I believe that ADC put me not only closer to the deceased but also closer to God."

For some survivors, these experiences are outside what they have formally learned in their religious educations. Specifically, the common perception or belief that a duality exists between the world of the living and the world of the dead is questioned. People who believe that "they are in heaven, over there, and we are on earth, over here" see the two realms as distinct and separate. For survivors, ADC provokes them to examine what they believe and leads them to conclude that life and death are less distinct than they thought. A widow who had dreams of her husband said, "Because of that experience I will not say that there's not another dimension out there. My mind is open to that. Whereas before I might have said, 'That's a little weird.' "

Rational Explanations

Within the rational explanations people use to make sense of their experiences, I found they often frame ADCs within a psychological or scientific context. What struck me most about the group of respondents who referred to themselves as rational thinkers is that although the experience didn't square with their rational worldview, none questioned their sanity. Not one person experienced the connection as a hallucination or as a symptom of a psychological disturbance.

Psychological Explanations

Initially many survivors accept ADCs on an intuitive level. They immediately recognize the truth of the experience through a nonrational way of knowing. However, over time survivors may turn to psychological explanations of ADC, which are rational constructs. When survivors find psychological explanations they are less sure that they have actually experienced the deceased. For example, Kerri, a psychological counselor, had vivid dreams of her husband after he died, which she immediately believed to be an experience of the deceased. As time went on, she began analyzing the dreams and started thinking about them as an emotional response to her grief rather than as a spiritual experience. She said, "I think about it on two different levels. On one level I second-guess it and think my mind created it out of a state of grief; on another level I know it's true. I think as I started pulling myself together, I put up the barriers and came up with a logical explanation."

It's interesting to note that everyone I talked to who subscribed to the psychological interpretation also simultaneously believed on another level that the experience was real. In fact the spiritual component remained constant but hidden. Some kept this belief hidden in fear of ridicule, while others kept it hidden because it was too private to share. What struck me was the survivors' depth of conviction that the experience was real underneath the psychological explanation. This belief accounts for the fact that none doubted his or her sanity. They were able to integrate the event as a positive, life-enhancing experience, rather than treat it as a psychotic episode.

Scientific Explanations

Another rational approach to interpreting ADC is the scientific perspective. When survivors analyze ADC scientifically, they often have difficulty accepting it. These survivors define reality as that which can be quantified. Their belief system leads them to reject their nonshared experiences as real.

I found this group to be the most conflicted because there was no way for them to quantitatively measure or prove the experience. But even for the most scientifically oriented, the experience held such a ring of truth that they were more inclined to discard their scientific beliefs than to discount the validity of their experience. Clinging to their old beliefs often created a tremendous amount of internal conflict.

For example, Todd, an environmental scientist, knew he had experienced something extraordinary, but he simply couldn't explain it. Surprisingly, he had not discussed his experience with anyone until we spoke. He was at a loss as to how to integrate this experience with his beliefs. He therefore compartmentalized it and had not received the level of benefit from it that I witnessed in survivors with a less rational approach. In fact, the clash of belief systems that the experience created for Todd caused him a considerable conflict, which suggests there are tremendous psychological benefits to be gained from a less rigid worldview.

Alan's story also underscores this point. Alan simply could not come up with a scientific explanation when he experienced a visit from his deceased uncle. The experience caused him a great deal of turmoil until he decided to change his worldview to accommodate the experience. "There was no way to explain it," he said "and because I believed it really happened, it made me more open-minded. I realized humans are so far from understanding the truth that I was a little foolish to think I had everything figured out."

When I asked Alan to reflect on how his new way of think-ing made him feel compared to the old, he said, "Happier. The world is a much more interesting place. Not that I go around making things up, I'm just not blocked to the possi-bilities anymore."

This view supports what I discovered in speaking to sur-vivors. The more creative and open-minded they were, the better they moved through their grief. Having a positive, spiritual outlook was a key component to both their accep-tance of the experience and their resolution of grief.

Rational and Intuitive Explanations

Survivors who can find both rational and intuitive expla-nations believe that subjective realities are just as significant as objective realities; they are merely different perspectives. I found this group to be remarkably resilient. They quickly reconciled the extraordinary by drawing from a broad range of concepts. This group was also highly creative in conceptu-alizing the world. Because these people did not adhere to one specific dogma, they created original internal realities that contributed to a strong sense of self. Unlike individuals with rigid belief systems, many in this group placed paranormal phenomenon squarely within the realm of science. They saw it as something science simply did not yet understand. They offered possible scientific explanations such as parallel uni-verses, subtle energy bodies, and theories supported by quantum physics. This group was also open to the idea that someday the phenomenon might stand up to the test of sci-ence. Seeing the entire universe as a spiritual place made these survivors more prone to weave science and spirituality into one.

For example, Beth, a bookseller, felt that she could explain ADC both spiritually and scientifically by relying on the principle of the construction of matter:

"You know if you think about it in terms of matter not being created or destroyed, but simply changing form, then it [ADC] makes sense scientifically. You know if you have ice and it gets warm, then it turns to liquid, and if it gets warmer still, then it turns to vapor. Our bodies are just matter, and they change form, too. When we die, we simply change form, and for some reason that we don't really understand yet, some people can experience those changed forms. Science can explain some of this, but there's still really a lot more to it than what we know."

Reconciling the Extraordinary

As survivors find explanations, they begin integrating their thinking about ADC. Although they know the experience is real on an intuitive level, it is important for them to find an explanation that fits with their construction of reality. Survivors are compelled to examine their belief systems and to abandon beliefs they had held until the time of the experience.

However, when survivors find it difficult to resolve their current belief systems with ADCs, talking about belief systems with someone who understands the phenomenon can be beneficial. The therapist can help them reexamine their belief systems and sort out which beliefs are still valid for them. For example, by examining which of their beliefs about death and life after death are limiting, they will be better able to see those that are life-affirming and growth-promoting.

Sometimes looking at the origin of beliefs is helpful. Long-held belief systems are often adopted as children without the benefits of critical thinking; these beliefs may include racism, sexism, ageism, and rigid scientific elitism. These forms of thinking all limit our worldview rather than expand it. The therapist can point out that the healthier course is to openly consider all possibilities in a nonjudgmental, compassionate way.

Once people come to some resolution regarding their private thoughts about the experience, they feel more comfortable when responding to the public reality.

For example, Joan had learned science from a rigid, quantitative perspective. She believed that if something could not be measured or counted, it probably was not real. She wanted science to establish the reality of her experience with her son. She knew she had experienced her dead son, and she desperately wanted her scientific way of thinking to fit with her intuitive feelings: "I know this happened; I just need it to make sense. I don't know how to explain to others what happened. It upsets me that this can't be explained from what I've learned in science." She was now confronted with examining her scientific assumptions and integrating them into her new way of thinking.

When Joan examined the origin of her beliefs, she found they came not only from her academic training but also from her parents. Furthermore, she found some beliefs held true for her while others no longer did. Consequently, she was able to discard those beliefs that no longer fit with her adult worldview. Joan finally reconciled her extraordinary experience with her scientific worldview when she could see the two as coexisting; one did not preclude the other.

Often, objective reality does not encapsulate the depth and breadth of human experience. Private, subjective realities, which are laden with emotional content, are often more meaningful than those realities that can be proven to be real by scientific methods. How real is a mother's love for her child? How real is the sorrow one feels from the death of a loved one? In fact, the most poignant events in life are experienced subjectively, and ADC is one of these experiences.

Seven

Responding to Public Reality

What Will Others Think?

𝓗*uman beings* are naturally social. We want to be accepted by others, and, in fact, feeling accepted by others is essential to our survival. Years ago, before I began my research, I heard a show on National Public Radio about a football player who recounted an incident in which he'd been doing a television interview with another player. During the interview, he said something to the other player like, "Have you ever had an experience on the field when you are right up next to another player and you can see energy around him and you can see it move before he does, so you know which way he's going to go?" The other player responded, "No, I've never had anything like that happen." But after the interview was over, the other player came up to him and said, "You know, that happens to me all the time."

This story impressed upon me how different our public selves can be from our private selves when we consider what others will think.

Lana, a science writer who lost her sister, said, "I can talk about this [ADC] from a scientific perspective; I can talk about this from a psychological perspective; I can talk about this from any perspective you want. The one that means the most to me though is the spiritual perspective. But since some people may not be able to relate to this, I don't always talk about it like that."

This type of self-censorship is a key component of the ADC phenomenon. Survivors are keenly aware that the non-sympathetic listener might categorize the experience as pathological. Therefore, they might "try out" different explanations until they develop several that could be drawn upon to suit specific audiences. However, it's important to note that survivors often create these multiple explanations first and foremost in an effort to reconcile the experience for themselves. Even individuals who said they experienced an instant sense of knowing might later entertain other explanations. These multiple explanations serve them well when they disclose their experience to the public.

After ADC, survivors not only have to process what has happened to them, but they have to deal with what they imagine the public response to their experience will be. They have to decide if ADC is something they can share with others, or if they'll have to keep it to themselves, knowing that secrets are often difficult and painful to keep.

I found that survivors were engaged in a tug-of-war between their private thoughts and what they thought would be acceptable to the public.

When survivors are reconciling their own beliefs, they are engaged in an internal dialogue: This is what I think. When they are reconciling their internal reality with public opinion, they are engaged in an internal critique: This is what I am supposed to think.

In their research paper "Phenomenological Reality and Post-Death Contact," Richard Kalish and David Reynolds discuss private reality versus group reality. They note that the writings of Carlos Castaneda have made people aware of "the importance of considering individual reality on its own terms as opposed to insisting that perceptions of reality must be shared in order to be considered valid." They also write: "Although such recognition is not completely of recent origin, behavioral scientists and other investigators have rarely permitted mystical, other-worldly, extrasensory occurrences to become part of their personal interpretation of the world. Unable to understand these experiences as perceived by the experiencing individual, they have found it difficult or even impossible to grasp fully the significance of their effects."

Though this paper is more than twenty years old, the scientific community has not progressed much toward accepting paranormal or mystical events. Because so little has been written in the scientific literature or the lay press that supports ADC, survivors believe the public response will be one of disbelief and disapproval. In her book *Fire in the Soul: A New Psychology of Spiritual Optimism*, Joan Borysenko, Ph.D., writes that the general public is more accepting of these types of experiences than are people who work in science or psychology. Borysenko believes things are beginning to change as "we let our mysticism out of the closet."

Within the therapeutic community, destigmatizing ADCs can only benefit the bereaved. However, recognizing that this perceived stigma does exist and that secrecy is a normal reaction to it is also important. As Sissela Bok states in her book, *Secrets*, "Control over secrecy provides a safety valve for individuals in the midst of communal life—some influence over transactions between the world of personal experience and the world shared with others. With no control over such exchanges, human beings would be unable to exercise choice about their lives."

It is imperative that those consoling the bereaved understand the sensitivity of the topic and not pressure the bereaved into disclosing more than their comfort level allows.

Moving Beyond Public Criticism

Survivors eventually reject public skepticism because they know their own experiences are real. First they reject it in a private way, maintaining their beliefs but not sharing those beliefs with others.

Marti is a homemaker who experienced her father. "It was so real. It was a very beautiful interaction, and I wasn't about to cheapen it by having someone tell me they didn't believe it." Another participant said, "You just don't go around talking about things like this, especially when it's something that's close to your heart. There is a good chance you'll get laughed at or told you're crazy."

These cases illustrate a common fear of denigrating the sacred and of protecting one's image. Denise, described below, illustrates how one survivor moved beyond her fear and risked criticism to share her story.

DENISE

Denise, a thirty-one-year-old gift-shop owner, lost her husband in a brutal holdup. One warm spring evening after a late movie, she and her husband, Jeff, decided to walk to a local downtown cafe. As they strolled down the street, a gang accosted them, severely beating her and stabbing her husband to death.

"They left me for dead," she said. "I didn't know what had happened until I regained consciousness later in the hospital. I was in shock for days. It was like having my heart ripped out. Words can't even explain how awful something so violent and so sudden feels."

For months Denise was, as she put it, "immobilized. I couldn't pull myself together to run the shop. I think I was hiding. My mom really got me through that crisis." The following year, on the anniversary of Jeff's death, Denise and her family and Jeff's family gathered at the site of Jeff's murder to pay their respects quietly.

"I didn't want to go at first, but I felt pressured into it. On the corner where Jeff had actually died, we left flowers and prayed. It was there that I felt his presence all around me. That night when I went home I was sitting in the TV room where the two of us always ate dinner. I was thinking of him when I saw him. I could see his reflection in the window, and it looked like he was sitting there watching TV with me. I wasn't scared. It was more like I thought to myself, 'At last. You're back. What took you so long?' except for a split second I was thinking he could actually stay with me, but then he was gone. We didn't say anything to each other. We just stared. But I knew he had come to thank me for going with his family to show my respects and thank me for praying. He would have seen that as a very big deal."

The next day Denise was faced with a dilemma. Jeff's twenty-two-year-old sister, Addy, confided in her that paying their respects to Jeff was merely to make themselves feel better. She said she didn't believe in life after death and that their gesture meant nothing to Jeff, who was gone forever. Denise struggled with the idea of disclosure. She knew if she revealed her secret to Jeff's sister, it would certainly get back to Jeff's parents. She feared they might even see her account as sacrilegious. However out of loyalty to Jeff, Denise told her sister-in-law.

As Denise said it, "I knew it was true, but I also knew that it sounded like I was going off the deep end. But she really knows me, so she would understand where I was coming from with it. In the long run, I told her because it felt like keeping it a secret was a betrayal of Jeff. It would be like he got murdered twice if I didn't tell her. And Jeff would have wanted me to comfort her in that way. I know his visit comforted me more than I can say."

Denise's decision to disclose was beneficial overall. Jeff's sister treated Denise kindly and understood her. Furthermore, Denise's sister-in-law convinced Denise to reveal the ADC to Jeff's mother, who was extremely open to the idea. By risking the negative opinion of others, Denise gained validation for her experience and gained a confidante in Jeff's mother.

At this phase in Denise's acceptance of Jeff's death, having an understanding listener was critical. In Denise's case, her decision to disclose meant she could move forward. Like many survivors she *entrusted*, rather than *trusted* her secret to a listener. She entrusted her secret to someone she knew to be kind and understanding. I use the word entrusted purposefully to point out the care in which the bereaved selects a listener. Denise used criteria that are quite common when choosing to disclose, particularly when it is uncertain whether the listener will be like-minded. The key criteria in these instances is how well the person knows and understands the discloser. In appraising the situation, Denise observed, "She really knows me, so she would understand where I was coming from with it."

As Dr. David Viscott states in his book *Risking*: "There is a difference between trusting and entrusting. Some people can be trusted not to hurt you, but are too insensitive to understand you. You entrust information that is important to you only to people who are sensitive."

In fact, the need to disclose is so strong that survivors may seek out individuals or groups in which they attribute the quality of sensitivity to the potential listeners.

The fact that Denise's reaction to Jeff's appearance was to question what took him so long is also of note. I've heard this from other survivors of tragedy, and I believe it may indicate a readiness to begin processing the tragedy and get on with life. A sudden need to move forward may be particularly pronounced in this group because tragedy can "freeze them in their tracks." It's simply too much to process. A great tragedy or trauma surrounding the events of a loved one's death can set the stage for the survivors to build particularly enduring psychological barriers to protect themselves from further pain.

In such cases I have seen ADC promote remarkable healings in the bereaved. One such survivor told me that when he saw his wife, he said, "Where've you been so long?" After that he knew it was time to get out in the world. "She was pushing me out," he said. "Telling me to get going. Plus, I had to talk to somebody about it. I couldn't keep her visit a secret."

Denise, too, was prompted into action through her ADC. And it was apparent that her way of moving forward would include Jeff. By not "betraying him" or denying his presence, Denise's resolution of grief was highly likely to revolve around a healthy internal dialogue with Jeff and a healthy external dialogue with his family. In this way the relationship with Jeff would clearly live even as Denise ventured back into the world.

How They Told Others

Disclosure is always a problem. All survivors selectively disclose their experiences, carefully choosing what and whom to tell. One woman had been raised to believe that only those who have died and gone to hell can have contact with the earth. Despite this belief, she was open to the concept of paranormal phenomena. She said of her selective disclosure: "There are people who would mean you harm if they knew you believed this. I certainly wouldn't just tell it to anybody."

In the *Archives of Psychiatric Nursing*, Barbara Limandri discusses the disclosure of stigmatizing conditions from the discloser's perspective. She found that the critical factor was the degree of stigma experienced by the discloser. Though the participants in my study did not have stigmatizing conditions, they did feel that society would not accept their experiences as normal. They were afraid that society would judge them as unstable. However, everyone felt that disclosure was important. They also knew that their disclosure would be within the context of a society that denies grief and does not openly sanction private realities of a paranormal nature.

Survivors share their experiences for different reasons. Most feel there is no socially sanctioned avenue for discussing this type of experience. Martha, whose experience of her grandmother was discussed earlier, was able to discuss ADC with her mother, who had also experienced Martha's grandmother: "We could talk about all these [paranormal] things, and she was not uncomfortable because she had actually seen a manifestation. She does not share that information with the ladies she goes to church with. I asked her that. I said, 'Have you ever told them about Grandmother?' and she said 'Oh no, I would not do that.' She doesn't know how to tell them so they would understand."

If survivors know their listener is sympathetic, they simply talk about ADC as they experienced it. Because it is real to them, they give an account of it as any other real events in their lives.

Some survivors feel the need to rationalize ADC when they talk about it. They want to make the experience credible to their listener, and sometimes to themselves. One woman said that even though she knew the experience was real, she felt foolish talking about it: "I think I've got to rationalize it. At a gut level, it's real, but if you can't rationalize it, it doesn't make sense." She went on to say that she was a little "embarrassed" to talk about spiritual topics. Some survivors give spiritual and rational explanations to let their listeners know that they can think about ADC intellectually as well. After describing her experiences with her mother, one woman said, "It has occurred to me that this is all inside me and that I'm projecting it out."

Survivors who accept two or more explanations of the experience are more apt to choose a rational, rather than a spiritual, explanation when talking to someone whose sympathy they are uncertain of. Even situations where survivors feel they have to rationalize ADC for their listeners help satisfy their need to share their experiences with others.

STEFFIE

Steffie, a seventy-two-year-old retired postal worker, was prepared for her husband's death. He'd suffered with a lingering cancer for years. "We were always going down to Sloane Kettering Hospital in Manhattan to get the latest experimental drugs. They worked for a short duration, but more often than not the cure was worse than the disease. The struggle got to be too much for Frank, and he made a conscious decision to stop all the experimental medications and the chemo. He went cold turkey. He was ready.

"He started doing much better for a couple of months, but I think he was just ready to go. He was at peace with the idea; I could tell, but it was so sad watching him slip away so quietly. He'd get up in the middle of the night and write in this little book. I thought it was his will, but later I found it was a diary. Mostly it was just an account of what he did, not so much what he thought. I didn't have to read that. I knew what he thought, same way he knew what I thought. His book was more about walks in the neighborhood, people he talked to, things he went to the store for. He was walking again, but I knew he was getting ready to go. He was so awful quiet those last weeks. That's the way he went, too. Quietly. He fell asleep and never woke up. The last thing he wrote in that book was, 'went to the store for pencils.' It broke my heart to see those brand-new pencils, never sharpened. So I hid them in a drawer. I didn't want to happen across them often.

"Several weeks later when I saw those pencils again is when I saw Frank. I picked up the pencils, and there he was at the desk, plain as day. The pencils triggered something in me. Maybe those pencils made me imagine Frank. It could be a mental association I made with the pencils; I didn't want them to remind me that Frankie was gone, so I turned those pencils into Frankie. Or maybe he was truly there. I think he was there if the truth be known."

Steffie's mixed message exemplifies the difficulties survivors feel in disclosing. By first offering an explanation that she thinks will satisfy the psychological community, she tempers the second explanation. I saw this disclosure approach used often in those reticent to tell. It's as if the discloser is feeling out the waters before jumping in. As we continued to talk, Steffie revealed more. "I say it might have been those pencils that triggered a hallucination, but if the truth be known, I don't believe that for a minute. Those pencils made me feel awful, and Frankie was back to make me feel better. I knew it was him the minute I saw him. I just felt him back in the room. We didn't have to talk because we knew how to read each other's minds. I knew what he was saying. "Enough with these pencils. Sharpen them and be done with it. That would be his way to tease me about being a sentimental fool."

Who They Told

Survivors only tell those they trust, or those they view as understanding. One woman told her sister, rather than her husband, about her experience because she felt that she and her sister had more compatible feelings about their mother than she and her husband had.

"When mom died, I felt pretty good about sharing it with my sister because we are so close. After I told her she told me about her experience, but that was more recently. It took her a while to tell me that she had an experience of that sort. If I'd told my husband, he would have had me committed."

Another woman said, "Basically I don't think of telling people other than my grandmother, because I don't feel close to them in the way that I do with my grandmother. We can converse about things like that, because it's something that has happened to both of us."

Why They Told

Survivors tell their stories for various reasons, and generally they are aware of the purpose of their telling. ADC is not discussed casually in conversation. Most people carefully consider what they are going to say and know why they are sharing it.

Some survivors need support and validation from others that their paranormal experiences are within the parameters of a "normal" paranormal experience. They also want others to share their experiences for the sake of comparison.

DALE

Dale's older brother, Tony, died in a car accident shortly before Dale graduated from high school. They had been extremely close and had planned on traveling across the country together over the summer. Dale was devastated by the loss of his brother. After the funeral Dale became depressed and despondent. He spent hours sleeping in an effort to dull the pain. His parents were extremely worried about him and coaxed him to see a therapist, but he refused. Day after day, he sought refuge in his dreams. One afternoon he had what he called a lucid dream where he and his brother met out on the open road. Dale was standing along an endless stretch of desert road when a form appeared in the distance as a mirage. Dale couldn't make out what it was so he walked toward the form. As he neared, he realized it was his brother. His brother asked him if he had remembered to bring the PowerBars.

Dale recalls his surprise at hearing his brother's question because in the dream Dale realized that Tony was dead. "I kept thinking in the dream, 'I'm dreaming so I need to ask Tony what it's like to be dead.' For some reason I never did though. Instead I asked him why he wanted PowerBars and he said, 'No, man, they're for you. You're going to need them on your trip.' "

Tony said he was startled awake, because he knew what his brother was telling him. "Tony was telling me to hit the road, before things got worse. I know he was right. I couldn't keep sleeping. Plus, I'd started to take my mom's Valium; I knew it was getting bad."

Two days after the dream, Dale hit the road. With a backpack and his camping gear, Dale embarked on the trip he and his brother had so carefully planned together for months. Dale said it surprised him to find that out on the road he wasn't lonely. "I thought I'd be lonelier than ever, but I wasn't lonely at all. Even when I was alone on a totally deserted road waiting to hitch a ride, I wasn't lonely. It took me about five states to figure it out, but there I was standing all by myself on some desolate road in Iowa when I realized I wasn't lonely because I wasn't alone. Tony had been at my side from the second I stepped out my front door. We'd planned this trip, and Tony was good to his word."

Dale went on to explain that when he finally arrived on the West Coast, he was overtaken with an uncontrollable compulsion to tell people about how he'd come all the way across the country with his brother Tony. However, he said he knew he couldn't. As good fortune would have it, Dale hitched a ride with a psychologist. Suddenly, he found himself telling the psychologist the entire story and all the events surrounding Tony's death. "I wanted to see how he'd react. He was really cool; he told me about another guy who this happened to. And he told me I was probably right not to tell all my rides that my dead brother was in the backseat. I think now that was an understatement. It was probably even stupid to tell him, but I just had to talk about Tony. Probably because when I was talking about him I felt him there even more. I could feel him in the backseat laughing his butt off at the psychologist's reaction."

Dale's compulsion to discuss his sense of presence was because of the recent nature of his brother's death; and at the same time he sought validation for the ADC.

One woman asked me questions about others' experiences while I was interviewing her and said she wanted to read my research upon completion to see if her experience was comparable.

Survivors want to know if their experiences are considered acceptable to others who have also had experiences or to those who understand ADC. As one woman said, "I just want to know that I'm okay." She needed approval from others, even though they were not "mainstream." But their need for sanctioning from others does not lead survivors to solicit approval from just anyone. Instead they only disclose to those they believe will be sympathetic.

Telling others is also a means of healing for survivors, an opportunity to express their grief in an uncensored way. Commonly, the bereaved feel compelled to talk about the events surrounding the death of their loved one. This obsessional review serves as catharsis and is therefore an integral part of the healing process.

Julia, a sales executive, said, "It helps keep them alive. You need to be able to talk to others about your new relationship with them. It will keep the healing going."

AVA

Ava's father died when she was away on a vacation with her boyfriend Mike. "I felt worse because I couldn't be with Dad at the end," she said. Nobody even knew where we were because my boyfriend and I took a secret trip to Mexico. The worst part is, it was a secret because Dad wouldn't have wanted us to go being unmarried and all. Ava told me she talked to Mike about her ADC because "talk is the only way to help me understand what happened."

Some survivors want others to know how interesting ADC is or to help them understand the nature of the experience. One such participant, a nursing student, told her class about her experience during a clinical conference.

Another man described his experience to a prayer group.

LENNY

Lenny, a fifty-two-year-old computer analyst, joined a prayer group immediately after an experience with ADC. "I was so amazed that something like this could happen that I wanted to share it and figure it out with like-minded people." Lenny's wife had been deceased for two years. He had not remarried and thought about her often. When she came to him, he said he was "shocked by the solid nature of the experience. She was absolutely there." Because the experience was not consistent with his current worldview or that of his friends, Lenny sought out a group of individuals who he believed would be sympathetic.

"In the prayer group people were receptive. They wanted to hear more, and I was extremely willing to discuss even the most minute details. They've helped me to see that she's reached the angelic fold. She can materialize to return to this plane. That would explain how solid she was. I could have dismissed the experience as imagined if she hadn't been so solid. But she was sitting next to me, and she reached out and took my hand. I feel so fortunate to have people willing to listen to me and help me analyze it. I couldn't explain this to the guys at work, and I certainly had to tell somebody."

When I spoke to Lenny, he was extremely excited about his ADC. However, he recognized the need to censor his disclosure at work. Limiting disclosure to a carefully selected group of listeners, particularly a prayer group or spiritual group, and excluding a less sympathetic group, such as coworkers, is quite common. Clearly Lenny's intentions in disclosing were to share his excitement and to make sense of his experience.

Eight

The Therapeutic Nature of ADC

I tell my patients, "Death alters relationships; it does not sever them. The physical body is gone but the personal relationship lives on inside you." Some of our most significant relationships with living people are with those whom we see infrequently. We maintain those relationships in our minds and in our hearts. Relationships never die, although they may change and grow with us.

I don't subscribe to the common notion held by many grief researchers that grief is completed when you extricate yourself from ties with the deceased. In his seminal paper "Mourning and Melancholia," Freud says the work of mourning is to transfer libidinal energy to a new love object.

I agree it's important to invest energy into an additional love in the physical world; however, I also believe it's important to maintain a loving relationship with the deceased. Furthermore, I believe you never truly let go. Instead you develop an internal spiritual relationship with them. This internal relationship has great power to hurt or to heal. One can bury past hurts only to have them resurface in unhealthy and unexpected ways, or one can confront the conflicts and resolve them. A relationship with the deceased provides the opportunity to resolve conflicts and allows an internal relationship to grow and evolve into a state of health.

BRIDGETTE

Bridgette couldn't understand why her mother never acknowledged her musical accomplishments more enthusiastically. She felt slighted until spiritual conversations with her mother revealed the truth to her. Through this ongoing relationship, she realized she was treated no differently than her sisters had been treated, and she realized it would have been unfair for her mother to single her out as the special one. Today Bridgette believes her mother's equal treatment of her accounts for her close, noncompetitive relationship with her sisters. Bridgette cherishes these relationships as her mother's gift to her. Instead of feeling slighted, Bridgette now feels blessed. Bridgette's ADC facilitated insight and therefore a healthier internal relationship with her mother.

In fact Bridgette says until her ADC, she looked for faults within herself that would have precipitated her mother's treatment. Her new way of thinking has also carried over into other relationships. Bridgette says she no longer jumps to the conclusion that she has done something wrong to deserve negative treatment. Although people may treat her badly at times, she is now more apt to examine the environment for external cues that might explain a person's behavior in a more positive way. If those cues do not provide an answer she says, "I'll actually stick up for myself. When Mom came back and we talked about my music, she said I should have talked to her and explained my feelings so she could have explained. I won't let things go like that again. I wish I could have figured this out before she died. But now is better than never."

Bridgette's description of her ADC brought to mind Dr. Martin Seligman's theory that a person's internal explanatory style greatly determines how happy and even how successful he or she will be. It is remarkable that Bridgette's negative internal dialogue changed so quickly after her experience with her mother. She went from being a person who automatically assumed guilt, quickly assigned blame, and generally interpreted events negatively to one who saw the world as a positive place full of hope. In short, Bridgette was transformed from a pessimist to an optimist literally overnight. This transformation is highly significant because as Seligman states, at the core of pessimism is a learned helplessness. Bridgette's realization that she can "speak up for herself" or control her environment will no doubt positively impact her life. And by framing the world more positively, Bridgette is a happier person.

Not all ADCs have an immediate therapeutic value, however. Some survivors take years to resolve internal conflicts, and some will never completely reach a resolution. Even though grief is a normal response to a loss, it is painful. Those studying grief generally view it as a process, occurring in stages or phases. My research revealed that ADCs often facilitate acceptance, the final phase of grieving. The comforting nature of so many of the messages received from the deceased encourage survivors to let go of the physical life they shared and move into a spiritual relationship with them. I was struck by the frequency with which people told me of messages from the deceased that said, "I'm all right." They also comforted survivors with the message that the survivor would also be "all right."

In addition, the sudden paradigm shift often challenges the survivor's worldview, abruptly creating a sense of awe and wonder and contributing to open-mindedness.

For example, Miriam said, "I was totally blown away. After I saw Mom like that, I had to question everything I believed. All of a sudden I started believing in God. I had gotten proof, so now I wasn't thinking about it in terms of blind faith. I also think I became more open to new ideas because mine had changed so fast."

On the other hand, those who were predisposed to a spiritual interpretation benefited from validation of their beliefs. Although it didn't alter their mind-sets, it often restored a sense of awe and wonder.

Joel said although his faith was strong, a visit from his deceased brother renewed his involvement in the church. "Boy did that ever send me running back to church," he laughed. "I really was always a believer, but now church is more meaningful to me."

Resolving Relationships

As I stated earlier, internal relationships do not die, which means neither do the conflicts associated with those relationships. When those conflicts remain buried in the unconscious they can create confusing and damaging emotions in the survivor. They may also surface in unhealthy ways, such as misdirected anger, self-pity, depression, anxiety, or in extreme cases, even psychosis. The goal of healing then becomes to confront those issues consciously, understand their origins, and resolve them. ADC facilitates this goal as illustrated in Bridgette's case and in Toni's below.

TONI

In life, Toni had a conflicted relationship with her mother. Now, years after her mother's death, Toni is still working to resolve their troubled relationship. As Toni explains: "I was twenty-four when my mother died. At the time she died we had a terrible relationship. My mother was an alcoholic. When she was happy, she was very happy. But sometimes she became paranoid. As a teenager, I did not realize what was really going on. The summer before she died she began hating three of her four children. She alienated us. She started going away; she would take off. One time we did not get her back. She went to another town and took an overdose. I really had trouble with her when she died. And I felt so guilty for that. After she was gone I began hearing her walking around the house. She wore those flip-flop shoes. It was unmistakable. I heard this for about a year. Then it evolved into seeing her. In a sense she was always with me.

"It took me about ten years to finally understand how much she suffered in this life. All those years I'd ask her why she did it, why she treated us so badly. She'd explained to me the level of her pain. It helped a lot to see it wasn't all about me and that I didn't provoke her in any way. I know how much she loves me now. She was just flawed like all of us. She's totally different now. I think of her as a wise, old sage. And she's been so helpful to me in that role. After she started visiting me and giving me this incredible advice, I started to change. Over time that change has been huge. I don't see things as totally bad anymore. I know there's good in people. There's good in my mother and in me too."

Again, we see how ADC holds the power to heal. The deceased can, and often do, help us delve into the unchartered territory of the unconscious and resolve internal struggles. ADCs hold the power to alter the negative into the positive; communication with the deceased can transform anger and hatred into forgiveness and love.

Another extremely healing aspect of ADCs is their power to maintain significant connections. In our culture individuation has become overly glorified. According to many prominent psychologists, the goal of self-actualization is individuation or separation itself. By making the individual the all important focus, our culture can minimize the psychological strength that connectedness offers. The disposable culture encourages people to move on when a relationship becomes troublesome. However, in not looking back, our place in the world can narrow to the point of alienation. We need to know where we came from and to respect our ancestors, including the deceased in our most immediate family. To forget where we came from is to forget who we are.

It is stating the obvious to say relationships could not exist without communication. However, this communication need not be explicit or verbal. The example of the relationship between the mother and child is a good one. Long before the child learns to speak, the pair form a powerful bond solely through nonverbal communication. Just as this nonverbal relationship flourishes at the beginning stages of life, I believe it endures after life as well.

In considering this concept, the work of D. W. Winnicott comes to mind because he explored the topic of emotional development, starting before birth and into early infancy. I've noted similarities between Winnicott's description of our earliest relationships and those we have with the deceased.

As Winnicott states, "Silent communication has to do with the very core of the self." He goes on to say that what the mother communicates on this level to her child is her reliability, while the child communicates his or her vitality. It's interesting to note these same characteristics in many of the nonverbal communications that transpire with the deceased.

For example, a common theme running throughout these communications are messages of reassurance from the loved one. Although these reassuring communications are nonverbal, their underlying message is one of reliability. The loved one is reliable; she or he has not left.

Leslie, a twenty-nine-year-old survivor, explained it this way: "The feeling of my mom's presence was so strong in that meeting that I felt completely confident. I wasn't scared. Knowing she was there with me made an amazing difference."

Ronald is a hiker who got lost in the woods with his young son until his deceased father helped him. "Once I sensed my dad was with us, I knew we would get back safely. Until I felt his presence, I honestly thought we might die from hypothermia. Instead, I rallied and thought of ways we could protect ourselves."

In both these examples the deceased sends a nonverbal message to the survivor that he or she is there for the survivor. The survivor, in turn, responds with vitality. As Ronald said, he "rallied." In this way our relationships beyond life closely mirror our relationships before birth and in early infancy, thus bringing us full circle.

In my private practice, I have noted a tremendous difference in the resiliency of those who intuit the reliability or enduring nature of their relationships and those who do not. Those who do not, appear to have a greater tendency to feel utterly alone. They also have more difficulty finding meaning in the universe and therefore in their lives.

AARON

Aaron, in his early forties, came to me with a presenting problem of uncontrollable anger and low self-esteem. He had had a series of failed relationships and had recently been terminated at work. Over the course of his therapy, it became apparent to both of us that he harbored a great deal of resentment toward his mother, whom he felt had abandoned him by dying. She died while Aaron was still a young boy. Even worse, Aaron blamed himself and thought he deserved to be abandoned because he had not been well behaved.

The psychological defenses Aaron created as a way of dealing with his mother's death further exacerbated his feeling of alienation and abandonment. Rather than endure any emotional pain, he simply suppressed all memory of his mother. As Aaron put it, "I erased her."

Of course Aaron wasn't able to "erase" the memory of his mother. It simply went underground. Unfortunately, when a negatively perceived relationship is suppressed, it often returns in negative ways, as in Aaron's case. The suppressed memory caused Aaron psychological pain for years until it became so disruptive he sought therapy. Without the insight to understand where his pathological behavior was coming from, Aaron angrily blamed the world for all his problems.

And he blamed himself on an unconscious level. In his view, he not only had been abandoned by an uncaring mother but also was an undeserving son. This belief came back to haunt Aaron in every relationship. Because Aaron viewed himself as the undeserving friend, the undeserving husband, and the undeserving employee, he unconsciously undermined each one of these relationships. Through his anger and uncontrolled impulses, Aaron actually made himself undeserving. I've seen this quite often in my private practice. A person's opinion of himself or herself can constitute a powerful self-fulfilling prophesy.

Fortunately, Aaron came to understand that it was not his fault that his mother died and that she had not abandoned him. He also began to see himself as someone who deserved good relationships. Although many see disconnecting from the deceased as the final stage in the resolution of grief, I have seen the opposite to be more healing. Survivors who continue the relationship, either through ADC or through a conscious effort to foster its growth, benefit immeasurably. They become aware of how unresolved issues are being played out with others in their lives.

In fact, when I first questioned Aaron about his relationship with his mother, he presented what might appear to be a healthy resolution to his grief. It was final, over, resolved. It wasn't until weeks later that he began to reveal the complete despair and shame he felt surrounding his mother's death. Had Aaron had the good fortune of an ADC experience with his deceased mother, I can only speculate on how it might have altered his life for the better. He would have had the opportunity to resolve many of the suppressed issues he wasn't aware of when he entered therapy. He would have been able to forgive himself and his mother. Instead, Aaron believed for years that his relationships were unreliable. In effect, Aaron lost his vitality the day his mother died. He began to regain that vitality once he resurrected her memory and faced his demons head-on. It is no wonder that Aaron had a string of failed relationships. He had not yet been able to resolve one of the most important relationships in his life.

I believe one of the greatest gifts ADC gives survivors is permission to revisit their relationships and change them for the better. Often this involves forgiveness, which can be a powerful healer. I believe that forgiveness is so healing because it is the process of letting go of anger, which is the great destroyer. I've seen this firsthand in my private practice, particularly in older patients who have held on to anger for decades. Anger has a strange way of taking on a life of its own and consuming a person. Sometimes patients may not even remember the initial source of their anger because it's been buried so long in the unconscious. Other times, I marvel at how clearly a patient recalls every detail of a slight or a mistreatment that happened more than fifty years ago. Both kinds of anger cripple, whether conscious or unconscious.

In contrast to Aaron's case, Jeb, in his early forties, had the good fortunate of ADC with his mother. His story was of immense interest to me because it was eerily similar to Aaron's. Jeb's mother had died when he was in grade school. Because Jeb was a wild boy, he believed his unruly behavior had caused his mother's death. As a defense mechanism, Jeb, too, "erased" his mother. He said he "never" thought about her until the day she appeared to him as he was finalizing a bitter divorce.

JEB

I first met Jeb in my office on a cool autumn day. He came to me, not as a therapy patient, but as a volunteer for my doctoral research on ADCs. Jeb, now in his early forties, had experienced ADC with his mother when he was in his late twenties. He had generously offered to share his experience with me for this book. As I learned more about Jeb's background, I was struck by the powerful catalyst ADC had been in fostering forgiveness. Before Jeb turned thirty, he had come to terms with many of the difficult issues surrounding his relationship with his mother, and ultimately his relationship to the world.

As Jeb recounts it, "First of all, I was pretty shocked. I hadn't believed in anything mystical at all. The first time I sensed my mom's presence was right after the divorce. My life had fallen apart, and I was on the verge of getting fired from a job I hated, so I didn't even care. Finalizing the divorce was like the last straw. I was sitting in the living room, shell-shocked, and I felt my mom's presence so strongly. She didn't say a thing the first time. But I got this weird sense that everything was cool. I can't tell you how grateful I was that she was there for me when I was at my lowest. Her presence set off all these memories of her. I hadn't thought of her in years, but all of a sudden I was remembering stuff she'd said when I was real small. 'You can do it, son.' Mom kind of stuff. But it struck such a note with me because at that moment I was ready to give up. I think I was even suicidal.

"I started remembering how mad I was when mom died. And I realized that I'd been mad at her all along. It came as a revelation to me. So after that I looked at it differently. I felt like things weren't hopeless and I probably wasn't that bad. At least I didn't have to be.

That's when I started turning my life around and made a decision to lighten up. It took a while, but something about that experience changed me. It was "cosmic." Jeb laughed.

He's right because inexplicably his experience gave him a sudden insight about the source of his troubles. That he could so successfully navigate such treacherous psychological waters alone was impressive to me. Reaching this level of insight can take a long time, and some people never achieve it. It pointed out to me the therapeutic power of the ADC experience. And as Jeb's story unfolded, I learned that later ADC experiences would serve as an inducement for Jeb's return to his church, where he found further comfort and spiritual nourishment.

Although Aaron's and Jeb's stories both have similar beginnings and happy endings, Jeb had the benefit of ADC, which acted as a catalyst. The insights came sooner, and the discovery was more poignant. Feeling his mother's presence helped him transcend old personal issues, move on with his life, and find spiritual guidance.

Easing the Grief of Other Deaths

Having an ADC not only can assist in therapeutic insights but also can help ease the grief of other deaths. Dee lost two people she loved dearly. Her grandmother died only a month before her father died. The experience with her grandmother helped ease her grief when her father died.

Dee said she grew up knowing God: "It was not until my father was gone that I really knew what that meant." Dee loved her father deeply, and she felt they were very much alike. However, she noted "He wasn't always easy to talk to. I loved him, but sometimes we battled."

DEE

Dee's father, Don, was a private man. But in 1991 he called the family together and told them his colon cancer had spread to his liver. The family's sadness was lessened by his resilience. Over the next year Dee accompanied him to his doctor's appointments and to his chemotherapy. Dee said, "I think the whole time he was working on himself spiritually. He started doing things to take care of mother and the house. He was preparing for his death."

As Don grew sicker, Dee discovered an inner strength she didn't know she had. She talked to her father openly. The first time she accepted he was dying, she called him on the phone, crying, to say, "Don't leave me." The second time she spoke to him about his death, it was face to face. She said they were so "connected" they could communicate almost without talking. Dee told him what it meant to her that he was leaving.

He responded, "You will always have me. I will always be there for you." At the time, these words seemed like comforting reassurance; now she fully

understands the spiritual meaning of what he was saying to her.

While her father was deteriorating physically, Dee
began to spend more time with her grandmother,
Mamie. She reassured her father that she was looking in
on his mother. Dee vividly recalls the last day she saw
her grandmother. It was in December, before
Christmas; she and her father had just been to the doctor's office. His liver was getting worse, and the
chemotherapy was no longer working. Don asked the
doctor, "Is there anything else you can do?" The doctor
responded, "No." Don accepted this quietly. On their
way home Dee asked her father if he would like to stop
at the nursing home to see his mother. He said he
would rather they just go home.

That evening, while Dee was at her parents' home,
she got a call from the nursing home. Mamie was not
doing well. Don was too weak to go, so Dee left to see
what she could do for her grandmother. In the mean-
time Don went to the closet and took out the suit he
wore to funerals, intuitively knowing his mother did
not have long to live.

When Dee got to the nursing home, she saw that her
grandmother was gravely ill. The staff wanted to move
her to the hospital, but Dee reminded them her grandmother had a living will. The staff proceeded to make
Mamie comfortable. At 6:10 P.M. Dee sat with her
grandmother, and even though she was unsure her
grandmother could hear her, Dee began talking. She
said through tears, "Mamie, you need to let go; go

home to the Lord. Your son is not far behind. Help pre-pare the way for him." At 6:20 Mamie died in Dee's arms. After his mother's death, Don began deteriorat-ing rapidly.

Dee said, "I became preoccupied with him, but he was never a burden. He was just the focus of my life at that point." She began staying over at her parents' house frequently because the situation was grave. At one point Don had to be hospitalized briefly for hem-orrhaging. Shortly after he returned home, the family called hospice in. Dee began to prepare herself for her father's death.

One day while she was driving home from work, a strong smell permeated her car. She said it was a sweet smell that she had never smelled before. She knew this smell was her grandmother. She loved the contact, but she was unsure of the significance. Later that evening she smelled her grandmother again. The smell perme-ated the house.

It lasted for about an hour, and Dee finally asked, "What do you want me to do?" Even though it was late, she knew she was supposed to call her mother and see how her father was doing. Her mother told her, "Your father's in bad shape." When Dee arrived at her par-ents' house, she recognized that he needed inpatient hospitalization at hospice. He was transported by ambulance. Dee was with Don when he died in hospice.

Because she had ADCs with Mamie, Dee was able to help her father with a peaceful death. As she pointed out, "If I didn't know Mamie was waiting to help him and that there was an afterlife, I wouldn't have had the courage to comfort Dad as he was dying. I would have been too scared. The worst part of that would have been he'd sense that fear."

In the days that followed, Dee experienced her father through dreams and a sense of his presence. These experiences further added to her sense of hope and helped to ease her through a terribly difficult time.

The therapeutic value of ADC cannot be denied.

Nine

The Healing Nature of Transcendent Experiences

The spiritual world has been very real to humans since the beginning of time. Our interpretations and images may change from age to age and culture to culture, but there has been a consistent belief that we are only a small piece of a much greater reality. And paradoxically this belief has made us feel safer and more significant.

Our connection to the spiritual realm fills us with a sense of hope so powerful that it has the potential to heal. Throughout my private practice and my work in hospitals, I have seen this connection firsthand. Other health-care professionals have witnessed this connection as well.

A 1995 study conducted at Dartmouth-Hitchcock Medical Center found that one of the strongest predictors of survival after open-heart surgery was the level of connectedness the patient felt to his or her spiritual practices. Other studies have found similar correlations, including a link between mental health and spirituality.

I believe it is this little understood connection between our physical and mental well-being and our spirituality that is at play when survivors benefit from ADC. At the core of this phenomenon may be the power that potential spiritual experiences, such as ADCs, have to promote optimistic worldviews. This attitude is highly significant because as Martin Seligman states:

". . . Twenty-five years of study has convinced me that if we habitually believe, as does the pessimist, that misfortune is our fault, is enduring, and will undermine everything we do, more of it will befall us than if we believe otherwise. I am also convinced that if we are in the grip of this view we will get depressed easily, we will accomplish less than our potential, and we will get physically sick more often. Pessimistic prophesies are self-fulfilling."

As I mentioned in chapter 1, the sudden nature of ADC creates a paradigm shift in the survivor. Often this new paradigm embraces a highly spiritual, highly optimistic outlook.

I also believe something else is at play, a healing force that's harder to define. Dr. Andrew Weil addresses this issue within the context of healing when he says in his book *Spontaneous Healing*, "We may marvel at stories of commonplace activities of the healing system, such as the repair of wounds. In fact, it is the ordinary day-to-day workings of the healing system that are the most extraordinary." He goes on to say that the body has an intrinsic ability to heal itself and that all bodies seek this balance of good health.

Although we now understand much about the nuts and bolts of how the body mends itself, we have little understanding of the mystical forces that trigger this mending. We do not understand the intelligence behind it. When it comes to healing psychological damage, we have far less understanding of the nuts and bolts and just as little understanding of the underlying mystical forces. But my research strongly suggests that ADCs dwell in this mystical realm along with other little-understood phenomena that dramatically affect our health. The sacred is truly everywhere, and it influences our well-being through our very connection to it.

And why wouldn't this be so? Why wouldn't such powerful mechanisms for emotional and spiritual healing exist along with those for physical healing? Given the body's propensity to heal itself, why would it not heal all of itself: emotional, physical, and spiritual? The answer is that the body does strive to heal all of itself. Illness is a reflection of an imbalance within the system. But science, in its never-ending quest to quantify unquantifiable systems into smaller and smaller bits, sometimes fails to recognize how one part of a system interacts with another. Today more and more solid scientific evidence confirms that there is a connection between the health of body, mind, and spirit.

From the intricate workings of the immune system to the restorative properties of transcendent experiences, such as ADCs, the entire healing phenomenon is enormously mystical. Anna's story reminds us of this.

ANNA

After the death of her husband, Anna, sixty-six years old, suffered from high blood pressure and depression. She also suffered from a series of colds and a serious bout with the flu that put her in the hospital with pneumonia. While in the hospital she had a dramatic ADC in which her husband appeared at her bedside. As she explained it:

"He was solid like you or me. When he bent over to kiss me on the cheek, I could feel his breath. Imagine that! He sat there and visited with me for about ten minutes, and he held my hand. His hand was warm and full of life, not icy the way you might think. He didn't say a word. I knew.

". . . I knew it wasn't my time yet. Morey was so at peace and so filled with happiness that I knew he would get along without me. I'd taken care of him for so long that I'd been terribly worried about him, thinking he might be frightened and alone. I know being alone frightened him. He always wanted me with him at the end, especially when he'd been so sick.

"Now it didn't matter. It's not that he didn't love me. It's just that now I knew you didn't miss people on that side because you don't truly leave them. Knowing that he was fine was such a blessing for me. And do you know what happened after that? I got well and I haven't been seriously sick since. My blood pressure even dropped. My doctor commented on that.

"That might not seem related, but I believe it is. After my experience with Morey, I felt stronger, so I buckled down and took control of finances, something I had relied on Morey to do. Seeing Morey again did bring it home that he was gone, doing well, and now I needed to stop worrying about him and take care of myself. I also began thanking God for taking care of him. Morey helped me find God in a more personal way. My time will come to join him, but for now I belong here with my children and grandchildren."

Anna's is a striking example of how ADCs heal our bodies, minds, and spirits. Her husband's visit was a powerful catalyst for change. Connecting to this little understood dimension brought Anna spiritual renewal, mental strength, and physical recovery.

In his book *Timeless Healing,* Dr. Herbert Benson eloquently speaks of the biological connection between spiritual belief and health. He states, "I believe that humans are wired for faith and that there is a special healing generated by people who rely on faith."

I believe this hardwiring describes our connection to the sacred intelligence underlying all healing. We are hardwired to a universal intelligence many call God. Our faith in this power helps us connect to it. I also believe the deceased connect us more closely to the fabric of this intelligence and to its sacred organizing properties. This may be because ADCs so often reinforce faith in believers, rekindle faith in those who have lost it, and create faith in those who never believed.

Hope as Healer

In discussing the healing nature of ADC, I must also address hope that builds a powerful bridge to the future. A belief system devoid of hope has the power to kill. The negative messages it sends to the brain make the body vulnerable to disease. Conversely, a hopeful belief system has the power to strengthen and heal. ADCs are full of hope.

At the root of the ADC experience is a message to the survivor that life is not meaningless or hopeless. It is sacred. And because death holds such fear for us, contact with the deceased allays a great deal of our fear. Because the deceased so often return with messages of peace and comfort, fear is replaced by joy in knowing that the survivor will once again be reunited with the beloved after death and that their union will be joyous and peaceful.

But something else is at work when we feel hopeful. For to be without hope is to be without a future. Hope embodies our dreams for the future and therefore our mental imagery of that future. Within the imagery of hope are powerful self-suggestions that manifest themselves in the physical world. Hope motivates us and propels us into the future in an exceedingly positive way. Rather than shrink from uncertainty, we embrace each day with a strength born of hope.

Dr. Herbert Benson has said of hope, ". . . faith and hope do possess considerable influence over us, and they are made physically manifest in a phenomenon called remembered wellness." The emotion of hope plays a key role, as in Lewis's case. I met Lewis the year after his wife died.

LEWIS

Lewis worked hard to provide for his wife and three children. For years he painted other people's houses. He hoped that someday he and his family would own a home of their own. "It kept me going. We'd go to Parade of Homes and look at the rich people's houses and picture ourselves there. It got me through the job thinking about it being worth something. Not for nothing." When Lewis's wife, Ruby, died of cancer, he was only twenty-seven with three children to raise alone. He lost all hope. "I don't know what happened to me, but I stopped believing in the Lord. I know I had the kids, but it was hard just getting out of bed on the weekends. When I did, I was finding my hope in a bottle. I was pretty upset that the Lord would take her from me so soon. I lost my faith. It didn't seem like a good world to me anymore. But then Ruby came down to me like an angel straight from heaven. She was so pretty and she told me everything would be all right. She explained that heaven was an amazing place. Ruby made me see that what happened to her wasn't bad, which made me feel a whole lot better about death itself. Besides, she made me see that being a good parent to the kids was a way to love her, so I'm doing that. And we all go to church and thank the Lord for what we do have instead of only looking at what we don't. The kids have good friends and things are looking up for me too because I've stopped drinking. We even started going to Parade of Homes again."

Lewis's story is a fitting example of how ADCs can restore hope and help the bereaved start looking to the future. The following story is also a dramatic example of the positive impact of ADC. In Brett's case, an ADC not only gave her a sense of comfort and hope about death but also helped her heal physically.

BRETT

After the death of her husband, Phil, Brett, a forty-eight-year-old speech therapist, developed eye problems. Her peripheral vision clouded. "Everything on the sides looked like it was smudged or there was a cloudy frame around it. When I looked off to the side, I had no peripheral vision. Nobody could find anything wrong with me. I even went to a neurologist. It was a horrible time . . . seeing Phil was what made me see clearly again. I'm not kidding. One night I heard a bang off to the left, so I instinctively looked over there. I thought it might be the cat, but instead I saw Phil, clear as day. My vision wasn't clouded. You would think I would have questioned the whole thing, but I didn't. I accepted it. I knew he was in the house. We'd been so close that I knew he was there for good. That night I had this wild dream that I was actually an eagle, and I could see all the way into the city from here. My vision was incredible.

"In the morning, I knew this was a very symbolic, healing dream; I wrote it down so I wouldn't forget it. I also knew Phil's presence in the house had something to do with my dream. Several weeks went by and I didn't see Phil. Then one night I was in the kitchen making popcorn, and the same thing happened. It sounded like something fell; I looked over to the side, and I saw Phil clearly. He was wearing an old pair of glasses. He took them off and put them in his shirt pocket. That's all he did. I knew exactly what it meant. He was telling me my eyes would get better. Up until that point I thought I would go blind. But, you know, I became less preoccupied with my eyes. I was so happy he was with me.

". . . every time I thought about the fact that he was dead, I was pretty scared. I had to stop myself from thinking about it because I would think the worst thoughts you can imagine. Very scary, like Edgar Allan Poe. But now there he was in the kitchen almost playfully letting me know my eyes would be okay. It was very comforting. The part that was the most comforting was the part about him being so happy. I'd wondered so much about death. I got myself so worked up with awful, awful thoughts. Seeing him and knowing he was happy was beyond words."

In Brett's case, her hope came from knowing both that her eyes would heal and that the afterlife was not the horrific place she had imagined. It is not surprising that Brett was able to heal; an ADC had filled her with hope and comfort. The fact that her husband had removed a pair of glasses to illustrate that Brett's eyes would heal and that it eventually happened exemplifies the healing capabilities of ADC. The actions of the deceased fostered hope for the future. By depicting a future for Brett without vision problems, ADC with her husband triggered her own inner-healing abilities; these abilities are greatly influenced by self-fulfilling prophesy. Brett's ADC transformed her from someone who thought she was going to go blind to someone who knew her eyes would get better. She went from feelings of hopelessness to feelings of hope, and in so doing she restored her vision. Brett now saw more clearly on a number of levels.

The Deceased Lead Us to Our Higher Selves

I believe these healing ideas come from an inexplicable connection to the deceased that also puts us in touch with our higher selves. These aspects help us shed light on how our symptoms or pathological behaviors are the expression of our unmet needs. Identifying these unmet needs, whether they be spiritual, mental, or physical, puts us on the path to fulfillment and happiness. For without the insight to identify our needs, we cannot take the necessary steps to fulfill them.

In private practice I am struck by how often patients hold themselves back because they do not know what they want. Their needs go unmet. Through therapy, these patients struggle and often work for months to tap into the higher wisdom of healing insights. However, many survivors who experience ADCs are blessed with such insights easily. I heard dozens of examples of how survivors went on to improve their lives after one ADC; the fifty-four-year-old uneducated widow who took over her husband's business successfully, the forty-three-year-old woman who stopped drinking and started taking care of her body, the thirty-one-year-old computer programmer who returned to a spiritual practice. In talking to these individuals, each described receiving a sudden insight through ADC that facilitated the fulfillment of a long unmet need: In the first case a need for mental challenge, in the second a need for physical health, and in the third a need for spiritual connection. And in all three cases, the deceased kindly but emphatically suggested how the survivor could better his or her life.

These insights came from a place of love and great wisdom so often characteristic of expanded awareness. In effect, we reach our higher selves with the deceased leading the way. Connection to our higher wisdom through ADCs may be explained through Jung's concept of the collective unconscious, for through this collective we can find all knowledge—including the combined wisdom of ourselves vis-à-vis our beloved deceased.

Heather's experience beautifully illustrates how the deceased lead us to our higher selves to help us tap our inner wisdom.

HEATHER

Heather, a talented artist in her late twenties, had been working two jobs to save enough money to attend a computer design school. During the day Heather worked at a bank for very little money. She was consistently passed over for promotions and saw no future in this uncreative, demanding job. Four evenings a week she worked long, late hours as a waitress in a restaurant and bar. She felt trapped in her struggle to save enough money to escape her plight. Heather calculated that it would take four more years to save enough money to quit her grueling schedule and attend the nine-month program. Although Heather had already been accepted to the program, she had deferred enrollment until she had the money.

One early evening when Heather was fortunate enough to have an evening off, she drove to the beach. There she sat on a large rock and watched the sandpipers dart back and forth, looking for their next meal. She thought how lucky they were to be so free. Their lives were so simple. Each meal was there for the taking. And the fear of debt was the farthest thing from their minds. No sooner had she completed that thought when she heard her mother's crystal-clear voice say, "Borrowed money is better than wasted time. Your father started his business with borrowed money." The voice sounded as if it were right next to her. It startled her so that she swung around full circle. But saw she was alone on this section of the beach, and just as she realized this, the most glorious sunset lit up the sky with brilliant color.

Heather instantly realized the wisdom of her mother's words. "I had absolutely refused to take out a loan, and ironically I made too much money for financial aid. But the more I thought about what my mom had said, the more my future opened up to me. Of course, I could take out a loan. There was tons of work for computer designers, and the money was so, so much better than what I was making now with two jobs. I'd have the loan paid off way before I'd save enough to go to school working these lousy jobs. As I was realizing all this, something else became clear. I'd been holding myself back out of fear. I'd actually been doubting my abilities to succeed. By putting myself on hold like that I could avoid failure. My future was on hold. But what I heard so clearly now was, 'You won't fail. When you put your mind and your heart into something you never fail.' That day I decided to start my future.

"I never would have figured all that out without my mom's help. It was like she started me thinking in the right direction. The next day, I set up a meeting at the school to talk to someone about a low-interest loan. All of a sudden, I wasn't stuck anymore. I got my momentum back, and my life turned around for the better from that day forward."

By gaining insight Heather was able to move forward. I think her statement, "That day I decided to start my future," embodies the spirit of so many ADCs. As one woman said, "I'd been frozen in fear, but it was like Jack gave me a quick kick in the butt. A nice kick." Although the idea of a swift kick from another dimension is a humorous one, it aptly illustrates how the deceased not only comfort us but also help us to reach potential.

The eminent psychologist William James made this observation: "I have no doubt whatever that most people live, whether physically, intellectually or morally, in a very restricted circle of their potential being. . . . We all have reservoirs of life to draw upon, of which we do not dream."

Through contact with another dimension, I believe we are closer to that dream. And I believe that realizing one's potential is an expression of health. Our glimpse into another reality helps us find the way to physical and emotional health, and it helps us transcend to a higher level of spiritual development. ADCs create an eternal bridge between us and our loved ones. They comfort us, they inspire us, and they heal us.

A close friend's stepfather died this year after a long fight with cancer. Although he had raised her, she never felt as if he truly loved or accepted her as his daughter. He died peacefully at home on Thanksgiving Day with his family around him. Because her stepfather was a hospice patient, she received follow-up counseling after his death. The hospice counselor helped her work through these issues.

During this time my friend vividly sensed her stepfather's presence. She knew I was writing a book about ADC, and she told me that she had something comforting to share. She said: "The most awesome thing I have come to realize is that you can feel more loved by someone after they're gone than when they're still alive."

This comment embodies a core truth of the ADC experience. Relationships never die. They continue to change and grow, and we continue to learn from them. Those we love never stop giving that love, and we never stop loving.

Many years ago someone said to me, "We are spirits in human bodies." That sounds like a simple concept, and it is. All truths are. Recognizing our spiritual natures adds layers of meaning to our lives and connects us to a universe full of awe and wonder.

The universe is indeed a magical place. Not long ago, few scientists would have recognized the link between human health and spirituality. But today scientists are embarking upon a fascinating journey to discover the relationship between spirituality and enhanced levels of well-being.

To paraphrase scientist J. B. S. Haldane: The universe is not only stranger than we imagine, it is stranger than we *can* imagine. Many of us may remember, as children, looking up at the stars and wondering, Where does it all end? and then realizing that we had proposed a question beyond our capabilities. We were confronted then with the fact that we could not fully comprehend our own reality.

Transcendent experiences open the door to a different realm, making the spiritual more accessible. ADC offers a key to this door, providing comfort and spiritual confirmation. For those who have not experienced the deceased, one of the survivors I spoke to said, "Just because you have not, does not mean you will not. The possibility exists."

Experiences of a transcendent nature not only show us the reality that exists far beyond our comprehension but also speak to us about our participation in it.

References

Andrade, C., Srinath, S., & Andrade, A. C. "True Hallucinations in Non-Psychotic States." *Canadian Journal of Psychiatry* 34(7), 1989, 704–706.

Benson, H. *Timeless Healing.* New York: Scribner, 1996.

Bok, S. *Secrets.* New York: Vintage Books, 1989.

Borysenko, J. *Fire in The Soul: A New Psychology of Spiritual Optimism.* New York: Warner Books, 1993.

American Psychiatric Association. *Diagnostic and Statistical Manual of Mental Disorders, Fourth Edition.* Washington, D.C.: American Psychiatric Association, 1994.

Freud, S. "Mourning and Melancholia." In J. Strachey (ed. and trans.), *The Standard Edition of the Complete Psychological Works of Sigmund Freud 14,* 124–140. New York: Liveright. 1957 (originally published 1917).

Harman, W. "Toward a Consciousness Metaphor in Science." *Noetic Sciences Review* 24, 1992, 35–37.

James, W. "Essays in Psychical Research." In *The Works of William James.* Cambridge, Mass: Harvard University Press, 1986.

Jung, C. G. *Memories, Dreams and Reflections.* New York: Random House, 1963.

Kalish, R., & Reynolds, D. "Phenomenological Reality and Post-Death Contact." *Journal for Scientific Study of Religion* 12, 1973, 209–221.

Lewis, C. S. *A Grief Observed.* New York: Bantam, 1970.

Limandri, B. "Disclosure of Stigmatizing Conditions: The Discloser's Perspective." *Archives of Psychiatric Nursing* 3(2), 1989, 69–78.

Stevenson, I. "Do We Need a New Word to Supplement Hallucination?" *American Journal of Psychiatry* 140(12), 1983, 1609–1611.

Viscott, D. *Risking.* New York: Pocket Books, 1977.

Weil, A. *Spontaneous Healing.* New York: Bantam, 1995.

Winnicott, D. W. *Boundary and Space: An Introduction to the Work of D. W. Winnicott,* New York: Runner-Mazel, 1981.